Also by Betty Rohde

So Fat, Low Fat, No Fat
More So Fat, Low Fat, No Fat

Italian
So Fat,
Low Fat,
No Fat

Betty Rohde

A FIRESIDE BOOK
PUBLISHED BY SIMON & SCHUSTER

FIRESIDE
Rockefeller Center
1230 Avenue of the Americas
New York, NY 10020

Designed by Elina D. Nudelman

Manufactured in the United States of America

1   3   5   7   9   10   8   6   4   2

Library of Congress Cataloging-in-Publication Data
Rohde, Betty.
Italian so fat, low fat, no fat / Betty Rohde.
p.   cm.
Includes index.
1. Low-fat diet—Recipes.   2. Cookery, Italian.   I. Title.
RM237.7.R626   1997
641.5'638—dc21   96-45247
CIP
ISBN 0-684-82920-7

This book is dedicated to Bob as always.
He is my tester,
my friend, my love, my partner,
my criticizer, my everything.

I appreciate his patience with my experimenting on him, and with
my absence from him since Simon & Schuster came along.
I appreciate his going along with me on trips as well as trying new tastes.
He never knows what he is going to have on his plate.
He is the greatest of sports; he is the greatest of husbands.
Bob, my love for you grows daily.

Contents

Introduction

■ ■ ■ ■ ■ ■

*I am appealing to the average American cook who enjoys cooking, all Ameri-*can as well as food of other nationalities—and that is what this book is about: Italian-inspired flavor. In other words, this is an Italian cookbook for everyone, with sometimes just a little American taste to some of the dishes. Even if this book is bought by native Italians who are looking to cut the fat and keep the flavor, I know they will enjoy just a little straying occasionally. So in these pages you may find just a few recipes for what I call my Southern-fried Italian dishes—of course fried without the fat.

I hope you enjoy the Italian dishes I have created for you with low or no fat. I hear from so many people that they love Italian but can't have it anymore because they are watching their fat intake. *Wrong!* Here it is: some of your favorite old-timers and many new-timers. Give them a try and see how much more you enjoy the flavor knowing they are without the fat.

I loved doing this book. I have come to love the Italian flavors even more than I thought I could. I have gotten a great deal of information that I had no idea I would ever even hear about concerning Italy, the Italians, their foods, customs, drinks, eating habits, lifestyles, and likes and dislikes regarding foods.

I thought that I was Fat, Fifty, and Finished. Let me be the first person to tell you that if you are thinking these thoughts, please read my books and be encouraged by me to go for whatever aspect you desire. If you need to lose some weight, if you want to cut the fat and cholesterol for health's sake, if you are a heart patient and have had fat, salt, and choles-terol taken out of your diet, if you just have something in the back of your mind that you would like to do in life and have thought impossible—please, think again.

I told you at an earlier time that my dad always told me I could do anything I wanted to do if I wanted to bad enough. Dad, you were right! I did take off the weight—66 pounds in 13 months; 40 pounds in the first 6 months—and have kept it off for over 4 years. I have lost as much as I weigh many times over, but I would just put it right back on as soon as I would go off whatever diet I would be on. What you have to do is to make up your mind. Once you have made up your mind, the battle is half done. Just start with "I am going to change the way I eat, the way I cook, the way I shop, and I am going to live healthier and happier." Believe me, when you take off a few pounds you are happier. Just looking in the mirror is a great experience.

I would go to the grocery store and spend two or more hours reading the labels, searching and having fun finding things I didn't even know were fat free. That was before all the shelves were full of fat-free items. Now it is so easy to fill your basket with fat-free that it only takes me a few minutes to do my shopping. I am used to what is where. I do always try to allow myself some extra time to look for new items of interest. There are new products on the shelf every day.

Don't be too hard on yourself. Start with cutting the fat, then add some exercise, then cut the portion size, then cut the sugar. Go into this easy; don't try to do it all the same day. If you do, you won't last two weeks! Don't be too hard on yourself.

I feel I have altered my diet enough to be healthy, and eat enough to be happy. I am thin enough to be healthy and fluffy enough to be happy.

Some Sound Advice

When I first lost my 66 pounds with fat-free cooking and eating, I never exercised. Now I try to walk to make sure I keep the weight off, because when your body becomes accustomed to a low-fat diet, you tend to eat more and can start to gain again. Exercise if you will, walk for sure, park a little farther away from the store or your office, walk briskly—the more you do, the better off you will be. Exercise also reduces hardening of the arteries, which occurs with age and, I am afraid to say, also increases the risk of high blood pressure and strokes.

Shopping for Groceries

Never shop when you are hungry. Leave 10 minutes for "search-out time" to search out new fat-free items or to read labels. Shop heavy on fruits and vegetables and light on meat.

Party

Never go to a party hungry. Eat before you leave home—fat-free, of course—and at the party, nibble on raw vegetables or drink some juice. Don't hang out near the food table. Be careful of alcohol; it breaks down the resistance to high-fat foods.

At the Table

Start your meal with a glass of water; it will help prevent overeating. Have soup for an appetizer; it helps to keep from overindulging in the main course.

Serving Size

Meat or fish should be served in portions about the size of a deck of cards. Normal vegetable or side dishes are served in ½- to ¾-cup amounts. Use small plates; it makes the servings look larger.

Say no to seconds. *Never* clean up your child's plate.

Motivation and Maintenance

Stop counting calories. My doctor told me to count my fat grams—that is where the calories come from.

A daily intake of 30 to 50 fat grams is average—I cut mine lower. You have to decide what you want to do and what is best for your lifestyle. If you find out what is easiest for you, you're more likely to stick with it.

Weigh yourself once a week, not every day. If you get on the scales twice a day you get disheartened if there are a few days without a number change. If you weigh yourself once a week, on the same day and at the same time, your surprise motivates you and delights you even more. You can't wait to tell your friends, "Wow, guess what—I'm down four pounds this week!" Wasn't that fun? Make it a fun and enjoyable process. I did and had a ball. Still am.

Socialize

Socialize with weight-conscious friends—you'll be less likely to overeat. I have a friend who is on a diet by my book and I feel very comfortable going to her house, as she does to mine.

Tips for Cutting the Fat

Snacking always seems to be the downfall of all. I know that one way I have managed to keep my weight down for four years is that I never felt like I had to starve or deprive myself of all the things I love to eat. I made up a way to make myself chips in the beginning, but now there are many low-fat chips on the market and no telling what else will be available by the time this book is printed in 1997.

You probably already know these tidbits, but it won't hurt to remind you, or maybe you are new to the game of cutting the fat. I hope you will remember these two words: PATIENCE and PERSISTENCE. These words will get you everywhere and help you to succeed in whatever you are starting to accomplish, be it weight control, job success, marital happiness—just about any area in which you are striving. Keep these words in your mind. If not for them, I would never have gotten the weight off to begin with. Can you imagine how many trashers I have had in writing these cookbooks? If I had let that bother me, I would have given up before I lost the first ten pounds.

Learning to cook fat-free is not hard. First you have to break the fry habit, as I have told you earlier—but do not put your skillet away. I use mine, especially the nonstick one, for many dishes. This is only one major way to cut back on fat in any dish you are making, be it one of my recipes or yours.

1. Spray your pan with vegetable cooking oil spray and leave out any other oil.

2. When baking, leave out the oil called for and substitute applesauce.

3. When you take out the fat, you take out the flavor, so increase the spices. Try adding a dash of cayenne pepper, a drop of red pepper sauce, a sprinkle of minced fresh chili peppers, a touch of cheese (fat-free)—for example, a sprinkle of Parmesan. Use green onions or leeks, green peppers, and tomatoes. When you're baking and take out the fat, add more spices—about 1½ times what the recipe calls for when you are modifying your own recipes.

4. Broil, bake, steam, grill, or dry-fry it. (Dry-frying uses only a trace of fat.)

5. Use egg substitute or 2 egg whites for every whole egg called for in whatever you are cooking.

6. Remove all the visible fat from any meat you're cooking.

7. Choose lean cuts of meat, poultry, or fish.

8. Substitute skim milk for regularly used milk, low-fat margarine or fat-free. Anywhere you can save a gram, save it.

9. Use mustards on sandwiches instead of mayonnaise; check the label for fat-free.

10. Use fat-free for regular salad dressings. Always ask for fat-free when eating out.

11. Use fat-free salad dressing for topping on your baked potato when eating out or at home. It is excellent. Also try salsa—on your baked potato, on your salad, as a dip. I know this is an Italian book, but you can still use salsas, and you'll find them in all stores.

12. Use herbs and spices instead of butter to enhance flavors.

13. Use skim buttermilk or skim milk to mash your potatoes. Add butter sprinkles or fat-free butter. Fluff them also with a little of the water you cooked them in.

14. Use onion for flavoring. Lay slices of onion on your baking pan instead of using oil to bake your fish or chicken. Sprinkle on dill or paprika and squeeze on a little lemon juice.

15. Pasta and beans are high-energy foods that don't leave you hungry in two hours.

16. Refrigerate stews, broths, or soups until the fat congeals, then lift it off. If time doesn't permit refrigeration, use a skimmer or gravy separator, or else a paper towel or leaf of lettuce to soak up surface oil.

17. Sauté means to cook quickly, fry fast. Instead of using oil, try water, or fat-free chicken broth, rice vinegar, Worcestershire, lime or lemon juice, or even wines. Always rely on your nonstick skillet.

18. Use potatoes to thicken soups or other dishes. Puréed, mashed, or instant potatoes can be used instead of creams in cream-type soups.

19. Fat is sometimes added for moisture. Instead, use fruit or vegetable juice or vinegar, wine, or beer.

20. Marinating: Instead of oils, try an acidic liquid such as tomato or citrus juice, vinegar, yogurt, or wine to go along with herbs.

21. Reduce sugar, when modifying your recipes, by one-third the amount called for.

22. Use ground turkey or chicken (fresh) instead of beef in your favorite recipes.

23. Use less meat and more vegetables in stews and soups.

24. Eliminate salt in any recipe except yeast breads. Enhance the flavor with herbs, spices, garlic, onions, citrus juices, and vinegars.

25. Try baked sweet potatoes instead of regular baking potatoes, which cry out for butter, sour cream, and the works. You'll have a sweet taste instead of the baked. Use fat-free margarine or butter sprinkles.

26. High-fiber cereals: Fat-free is a great way to start the day. Add skim milk and you're off to a great start.

27. Bagels are great anytime. If I am running, I take along bagels—the little tiny ones—and munch along the way. This staves off the hunger overeating urge when I do eat.

28. If you feel hungry, try drinking a glass of water, even a flavored seltzer type.

29. Eat an orange when the hunger hits. Take your time peeling and eating. You'll feel great to know you have eaten something so good for you, and your hunger is gone. You even gave yourself a shot of vitamin C.

30. To avoid binges, indulge yourself once in a while. Eat a low-fat candy bar, slowly, because they are small, and enjoy it as long as you can. You'll have taken in less fat and calories than if you had eaten a piece of cake or ice cream, but then if you are paying attention, you could have your cake and eat it too. Just make sure it is fat-free.

31. Season with vinegars. Since beginning work on this Italian book, I have found a whole new world of vinegars. It's been like the search for fat-free items when I first started. Every market I go to seems to carry different ones. Balsamic vinegar is great. Then there are garlic-flavored, wine-flavored, and all sorts of other vinegars too numerous to name.

GLOSSARY

Arborio.
The generic name of the most commonly imported variety of Italian rice. It is available under many name brands and is sold at many food shops in department stores and of course Italian groceries.

Balsamic vinegar.
A wonderful flavor resulting from the aging and reduction of white Trebbiano grape juice. You can just sprinkle it over almost everything.

Biscotti.
Italian for twice-baked cookies, to dip in coffee, tea, wine, or just for plain eating.

Biscotti dipping wine.
Vin Santo, the best, comes from Tuscany.

Burro.
Italian for butter.

Fresh herbs.
To store fresh herbs, wrap the stems in a damp paper towel, place in a plastic bag, and refrigerate. Or put the stems in a glass of water like a bouquet and refrigerate.

Fritta.
Italian for fried.

Herbed vinegar.
Made with fresh herbs such as basil, tarragon, and dill steeped in vinegar for a period of time. You can find a wide variety of wonderful vinegars in large grocery stores; two of them are in Gore, America.

Parsley.
Italian parsley is larger, with less curly leaves than regular parsley. For Italian cooking you really should use Italian parsley, but if it is not available, don't worry. The regular variety is quite satisfactory.

Pine nuts (pignoli).
Very high in fat; found inside the pine cones from different varieties of pine trees in China, Italy, Mexico, North Africa, and Southwestern United States.

Rice (riso).
Italian rice is thicker and shorter than American rice; it takes a little longer to cook, but it has a little more body. It is good in risotto because the grains adhere nicely without losing their firmness. It is excellent for Italian soups.

Ricotta.
A soft, bland, white milk product made from whey (white watery part that separates from the curd). Famous for ricotta cheesecakes; used in pasta fillings.

Risotto.
A creamy Northern Italian rice dish high in starch. Arborio rice is the preferred variety for risotto.

Salt.
Almost all canned beans and vegetables have more salt than we need. Almost always rinse them before using to remove some of the salt.

Spinach.
A great source of iron plus vitamins A and C. I hope you read my spinach story in *More So Fat, Low Fat, No Fat*, which came out in 1996. I had to eat spinach for iron when I was a child. Good thing Dad raised it.

Sun-dried tomatoes.
May be purchased in oil or dry-packed in cellophane, and sometimes loose (as I found them in New York). Guess which ones to buy. No—not the ones in oil! The ones that are just dried. Soak them in warm water before using.

Soups,
Salads,
and
Dips

Two Short Blocks to Red Pepper Soup

When asked by Simon & Schuster to do an Italian book, I thought OK! Now you probably already know where I live from the previous books, *So Fat, Low Fat, No Fat* and *More So Fat, Low Fat, No Fat.* If not, let me tell you.

Gore, Oklahoma, which I refer to as Gore, America, is a wonderful small town of about 670 people, very clean, friendly, and small. This is a resort-area town, pathway to Lake Tenkiller, which draws a large number of area city dwellers annually. Nevertheless, I still live in a small town. I pride myself on the fact that all the ingredients in my previous books could be found in our one grocery store, making it easy for readers to use the recipes. I have had comments from one side of the States to the other, as well as Canada. You would be surprised at the number of phone calls I get every day from ladies all over, referring to the simplicity of the ingredients in my recipes. One lady called me just yesterday and I didn't get her name and address, which I am sorry for because I like to write to some of my callers.

I had gotten into this book about halfway when I discussed the ingredients with my editor. She said, "You are now international, so you need to get out of town." Ha! She was telling me to go to the nearest city and to a larger grocery store for a larger selection. I did, I really did. I took three other ladies and flew to *New York City.* Now, how is that for getting out of town? Don't tell *me* to go somewhere.

I am going to tell you about Two Short Blocks to Red Pepper Soup, starting with the entire ordeal from takeoff to return.

Two of us were flying on one airline and the other two were supposed to be an hour behind us on another airline. I had forgotten to advise the other ladies of our flight number and I tried all the previous evening to reach them because something told me they were going to land in New York City before us, even though this was not the schedule. They traveled to Tulsa to spend the night before leaving because of such an early departure the next morning. I could *not* find them. Departure time: We board, taxi out to runway, taxi back. Problem with aircraft. The captain advised us it would only be a few minutes' delay. I tried desperately to send a message to Ann, because I knew they were at their gate awaiting their departure. An hour later we watched their aircraft leave. Another hour and our aircraft left. I don't even need to tell you that we missed our connection in Atlanta. Rushed to another gate with a flight leaving in five minutes. Have you ever been in the Atlanta airport? No other words needed! We got on, in the back, made it to New York OK.

We had to go out front of the airport, catch a bus that would take us around to the airline that Ann and Cleo came in on. Finally we got there. I went up to the information desk to have them paged, and this lady (Cleo —whom I had never met before) overheard me saying Ann's name and said, "Are you Betty?" They were standing, ready to kill me as well as leave me and go into the city.

I knew that the limousine that was scheduled to pick us up was going to be a problem because of the delays. It was, it was, it was. He *left!* I don't think I should have to tell you I was on the phone loud and clear. Five times to be exact. The operator kept telling me to deposit another nickel. I had everything except nickels. I could see the girls, I kept waving for them to come and bring me change. They kept waving back. Guess they thought I was so happy to see them I just kept waving at them. Finally after one hour and fifteen minutes our limo arrived.

Four Okies standing on the street in the rain at New York City airport. Got your attention? Just wait, it only gets better. Remember, we have just arrived. We are finally in the limo and on our way to our hotel. It is now 7:15 P.M. We have tickets for *Showboat* at 8:00. Are we going to make it? Nope! When we finally got to our rooms it was ten minutes until 8:00. I told the ladies, "You have ten minutes to change." Well, Cleo had this bad hair day; nothing more need be mentioned. We ask directions to the theater. Just *two short blocks.* Three of us had umbrellas, and we started walking, which is what everyone in New York does. Oops, we overshot— we have gone six blocks; got to go back. It seems that when it starts to sprinkle in New York, like magic, the umbrella vendors just appear on the street corners. Ann bought herself an umbrella for five dollars. Does that tell you how large it was? It would just about cover a postage stamp. We arrived at the theater sixteen minutes late; our seats were fantastic; we were wet, cold, and hungry. I forgot to tell you we didn't get anything other than pretzels and Coke since our breakfast at 7:00 A.M. I was all right except for my legs; my hose were sopping wet, my legs were trembling.

The show was so fantastic that I forgot about being wet, cold, and hungry. When we started our walk back to the hotel, it was pouring even harder, I mean really pouring. We were met on a corner by a limousine and asked if we wanted a car. Guess what our answer was. You got it, *Yes! Just two short blocks.* When we arrived at the hotel we headed for the restaurant. They were serving an after-theater menu by this time, one of the items being Roasted Red Pepper Soup. To cold, wet, hungry ladies that sounded good. Now, "good" is not the word. It was great. Cleo had to have Pepper Soup every night we were there.

Day Two of the trip: We were to be picked up by an escort from Simon & Schuster (Erin) to do research for the Italian book in Little Italy, Greenwich Village, etc. A tour you have never seen the likes of. She took us into specialty shops that I never knew existed. Spice shops, sausage shops, cheese shops, markets, to a real Italian restaurant for lunch. We all ordered different things so I could taste the different Italian seasonings. Then there were the pastries. I never saw such beautiful pastries. I did taste a couple, but I know I must have gained three pounds just looking through the windows of the shops. I drooled, to say the least.

We really had a great time—wonderful food shopping and research a success. Hotel, dressed, theater, Red Pepper Soup. (I couldn't eat it—too much cream and too many fat grams swimming around in there.)

Third day, everywhere we start to go, we are *"just two short blocks."* We'd heard that all day the day before; we walked and walked, which is why so few New Yorkers are overweight and so many are in good health: they walk everywhere and think nothing of it. "Just two short blocks" may be seven or eight blocks.

Today we are going to *ride* those little short blocks. We did. Great day of shopping in New York City. Cleo bought some men's cologne and was given *another umbrella.* This one was a long one; we had to treat it like a piece of luggage on the return trip. It got to be a real joke about this umbrella, just because it was a gift. If it had been for sale, there is no way she would have brought it home. She could probably buy the factory, but she hung on to this free umbrella. (I forgot to tell you: Ann bought another automatic fold-up umbrella. Now there are four of us and *SIX* umbrellas.)

Theater, Red Pepper Soup. Ladies, how's that for getting out of town?

Day Four started with a horse-drawn buggy ride in Central Park. Brunch at Tavern on the Green, back to the hotel, pack, had thirteen pieces of luggage and one umbrella, to airport and home. What a wonderful trip! Sure wish I had the recipe for the Roasted Red Pepper Soup. If you have one, please send it to me.

MINESTRONE

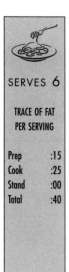

SERVES 6

TRACE OF FAT PER SERVING

Prep	:15
Cook	:25
Stand	:00
Total	:40

1¼ cups chopped onion
1 clove garlic, crushed
1¼ cups water
1 cup sliced celery
1 (8-ounce) can whole-kernel corn, undrained
1 cup sliced zucchini
1 (8-ounce) can kidney beans, undrained
1 cup small-diced cabbage
1 (28-ounce) can whole tomatoes, undrained
½ cup uncooked elbow macaroni or any small pasta
2 teaspoons instant chicken bouillon granules
1 teaspoon Italian seasoning

In a deep nonstick dutch oven or saucepan, sauté the onion and garlic in about ¼ cup of water just until crisp-tender. Stir in the remaining cup of water, the celery, corn, zucchini, kidney beans, cabbage, and tomatoes, breaking up the tomatoes with a fork or knife. Heat to boiling. Add the macaroni, bouillon, and seasoning and return to a boil. Reduce the heat and simmer, stirring occasionally, until the macaroni is tender, about 25 to 30 minutes.

Turkey Minestrone:

Use lean ground turkey and cook with the onion and garlic. Place in a colander and rinse with hot water to rinse away any excess fat. Clean the pan; return the turkey mixture to the pan and continue with the recipe.

Thyme

🌿 The word "thyme" comes from a Greek word that means "to fumigate." Its use dates back to the ancient Greeks. Sometimes thyme is called "poor man's herb" because of the ease with which it can be grown. A perennial, it can grow about one foot tall in any average soil, but it does require heat and good drainage. If you're ever in doubt about which herb to use, choose thyme. Best with grilled, roasted, or broiled meat, it also brings out the flavor in many vegetables, soups, and fish dishes.

PASTA AND VEGETABLE SOUP

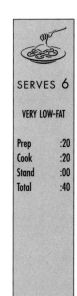

SERVES 6

VERY LOW-FAT

Prep	:20
Cook	:20
Stand	:00
Total	:40

³/₄ cup chopped onion
2 cloves garlic, minced
1¼ cups chopped 99% fat-free ham
1 teaspoon dried oregano leaves
½ teaspoon dried thyme leaves
Dash of pepper
1 (16-ounce) can whole tomatoes, undrained
1 cup uncooked elbow macaroni
2 medium potatoes, peeled and cut into small pieces
1 (15-ounce) can Great Northern beans, drained and rinsed
1 small zucchini, thinly sliced
Fat-free Parmesan cheese for garnish (optional)

Sauté the onion and garlic in ¼ cup of water in a nonstick dutch oven or large saucepan just until crisp-tender. Add the ham and continue to cook for a couple of minutes, stirring to blend. Stir in about 3 cups of water, the oregano, thyme, pepper, and tomatoes. Break up the tomatoes with a wooden spoon. Heat the mixture to boiling.

Stir in the macaroni and potatoes; reduce the heat and continue to cook until the macaroni is just tender, about 10 to 12 minutes. Stir in the beans and zucchini; continue to cook until the zucchini is crisp-tender, about 3 to 4 more minutes. When serving, sprinkle Parmesan over the soup if desired.

CHICKEN VEGETABLE SOUP

This looks like a long recipe but it's just all the spices.

SERVES 8

.50 GRAMS FAT
PER SERVING

Prep	:15
Cook	:45
Stand	:00
Total	1:00

8 chicken tenders
1 clove garlic, minced
1/4 teaspoon Italian seasoning
1/4 teaspoon lemon pepper
1/8 teaspoon crushed rosemary leaves
1/8 teaspoon crushed sage leaves
1/8 teaspoon oregano leaves
1/8 teaspoon celery seed
1/8 teaspoon crushed basil leaves
2 cups diced peeled potatoes
1 1/2 cups okra, trimmed and sliced
1 tablespoon vinegar
1 (14-ounce) can fat-free chicken broth
3/4 cup chopped onion
1 cup chopped celery
1 1/2 cups broccoli cuts
3/4 cup frozen corn kernels
1 cup diced or sliced carrots
1 (16-ounce) can green beans, drained

Cover the chicken tenders with water in a large saucepan. Bring to a boil and add the garlic, Italian seasoning, lemon pepper, rosemary, sage, oregano, celery seed, and basil. Reduce the heat and simmer until the chicken is tender, about 20 minutes.

Meanwhile, chop and prepare the vegetables. (Cover the potatoes with water to keep them from turning dark; drain before using.)

In a separate medium-size saucepan, cover the okra with water. Add the vinegar and cook until crisp-tender, about 4 minutes. Drain in a colander, rinse with hot water, and set aside.

When the chicken is tender, remove it from the broth with a long-handled fork and, when cool enough to handle, chop into bite-size pieces. Add the chicken broth to the saucepan, along with the onion, celery, broccoli, corn, carrots, and potatoes. Cook for about 10 minutes; add the okra and green beans and return the chicken to the pan. Continue to cook until all the vegetables are tender. Don't stir too much; it will mush up your vegetables and chicken.

POTATO AND ONION SOUP

3 to 4 cups diced peeled potatoes (¼-inch cubes)
1 large yellow onion, peeled and chopped fine
3 to 4 cups water
½ cup chicken bouillon granules
Salt and pepper to taste
Skim milk (optional)
Fat-free Parmesan cheese

SERVES	6
0 GRAMS FAT	
Prep	:10
Cook	:35
Stand	:00
Total	:45

In a large saucepan, cover the potatoes and onion with the water and chicken bouillon. Bring to a boil, lower the heat, and simmer until the potatoes and onions are tender. With a potato masher, mash about half the potatoes. Add salt and pepper to taste and continue simmering until thickened. If too thick, add a little skim milk—this is a soup. Serve with Parmesan sprinkled over each serving.

ZUCCHINI AND ARBORIO RICE SOUP

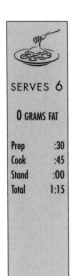

SERVES 6

0 GRAMS FAT

Prep	:30
Cook	:45
Stand	:00
Total	1:15

1 medium onion, chopped
1 clove garlic, minced
3 medium zucchini, cut into ½-inch cubes (about 1½ pounds)
2 teaspoons salt
¼ teaspoon pepper
Dash of freshly grated nutmeg (about ¼ teaspoon or less)
1½ cups chopped fresh or canned plum tomatoes, drained
6 cups fat-free vegetable broth (about 2½ or 3 cans)
1 cup arborio rice
2 tablespoons finely chopped parsley
2 tablespoons finely chopped fresh basil
1 teaspoon grated fat-free Parmesan cheese

In a large nonstick saucepan, cook the onion and garlic in ¼ cup of water over low heat, stirring, until softened but not browned, about 6 or 7 minutes. Add the zucchini and season with the salt, pepper, and nutmeg. Increase the heat to medium and cook, stirring, until the zucchini is barely tender, about 10 minutes. (You may need to add a little water to keep it from getting too dry.)

Add the tomatoes, vegetable broth, rice, parsley, and basil. Increase the heat to moderately high and bring the soup to a boil. Reduce the heat to low and simmer until the rice is tender, about 20 minutes. Serve hot or at room temperature, with Parmesan cheese sprinkled over each serving.

CANNELLINI BEAN SOUP

A quick and easy recipe for cold winter nights.

2 (15-ounce) cans cannellini (white kidney beans), undrained
2 bean cans water
¾ cup chopped onions
¼ cup chopped green pepper
½ cup chopped celery
Salt and pepper to taste

In a medium-size heavy sauce pan, combine the beans and water. Start to cook over medium-high heat. Meanwhile, in a non-stick skillet, sauté the onion, green pepper, and celery in ¼ cup water until crisp-tender. Add the sautéed vegetables to the beans and water, bring up to a boil, lower the heat, and simmer for about 30 minutes. At this time, mash the beans and vegetables with a potato masher until only small pieces remain. This will thicken the soup. Lower the heat and simmer for about 10 additional minutes, stirring often.

Note: If you like your soup a little thicker, you may add about 3 to 4 table-spoons of instant potato flakes, stirring as you add; then simmer just a little longer until the soup has the desired thickness.

SERVES 4

LESS THAN 1.75
GRAMS FAT
ENTIRE RECIPE

Prep	:12
Cook	:40
Stand	:00
Total	:52

LAYERED RICE SALAD

SERVES 8

1 GRAM FAT
PER SERVING

Prep	:25
Cook	:05
Stand	1:05
Total	1:35

1½ cups instant rice or 3 cups leftover cooked rice
3 cups shredded lettuce—your choice
1 small red onion, sliced thin and separated into rings
1 (10-ounce) package frozen green peas, thawed
1 (15-ounce) can cannellini (white kidney beans), drained and rinsed
  (see Note)
1 cup fat-free Italian salad dressing

In a medium-size saucepan, bring 1½ cups of water to a boil, add the rice, cover, and remove from heat. Let stand about 5 minutes; fluff with a fork.

Choose a nice large clear-glass bowl, like a trifle bowl or just a straight-sided salad bowl. (It needs to be straight up and down because you will need to dip straight up and down when serving.) Cover the bottom with about 1 cup of the shredded lettuce. Add half the onion, half the rice, all the green peas, another cup of lettuce, the remaining onion, the remaining rice, and all the cannellini. End with a small mound of lettuce on the top. Cover and chill. About 1 hour before serving, pour the dressing evenly over the salad, cover, and continue to chill.

When serving, dip straight up and down with a salad fork and spoon in order to serve ingredients evenly.

Note: You can substitute Great Northern beans for the cannellini.

MAMMA'S MACARONI SALAD

3 cups uncooked medium macaroni (Mamma used elbow shape)
3 medium-size tomatoes, cut into dice
¼ cup sliced stuffed olives (about 12 olives)
½ cup chopped onion
¾ cup chopped green pepper
1½ to 2 cups fat-free Italian salad dressing

Cook the macaroni as directed on the package, drain, rinse with cold water, and drain again. In a large bowl, mix the tomatoes, olive slices, onion, and green pepper. Stir in the macaroni and enough salad dressing to coat evenly. Let stand about 1 hour before serving to let the flavors blend.

Variation:

If you are making this ahead, just place the macaroni on top of the mixed vegetables; do not stir. Cover and refrigerate until about 1 hour before using. Add the dressing, stir, and let stand about 1 hour to blend the flavors.

SERVES 8

.75 GRAMS FAT
PER SERVING

Prep	:25
Cook	:00
Stand	1:00
Total	1:25

TOMATO-PASTA SALAD

SERVES 6

2 GRAMS FAT
PER SERVING

Prep	:12
Cook	:00
Stand	2:00
Total	2:12

2 cups chopped ripe tomatoes
2 green onions with tops, chopped
2 cloves garlic, minced
2 tablespoons minced parsley
1 teaspoon light olive oil
¼ teaspoon salt
½ teaspoon dried basil
⅛ teaspoon coarse black pepper
1 (7-ounce) package macaroni shells, cooked according to package
    directions, drained, and cooled.

In a bowl with a lid, mix the tomatoes, onions, garlic, parsley, oil, salt, basil, and pepper. Toss with the macaroni, cover, and refrigerate for at least 2 hours before serving.

ZESTY PASTA SALAD

SERVES 6

LESS THAN
1 GRAM FAT
PER SERVING

Prep	:20
Cook	:25
Stand	2:00
Total	2:45

1¼ cups broccoli florets, steamed until crisp-tender
½ cup chopped green pepper
½ cup chopped tomato
¼ cup green onion slices
2½ cups corkscrew noodles, or any type of pasta, cooked and
    drained
¾ cup fat-free zesty Italian salad dressing
¾ cup fat-free mayonnaise, such as Miracle Whip

In a large salad bowl, mix the broccoli, pepper, tomato, onion, and pasta. Toss lightly. In a small separate bowl, combine the two dressings. Stir with a wire whisk until blended. Pour over the pasta mixture. Toss gently to combine well. Cover and chill for at least 2 hours before serving to let the flavors blend.

ROTINI GARDEN SALAD

1 cup chopped zucchini
1 cup sliced fresh mushrooms
1 (15¼-ounce) can green lima beans, drained
1 small green pepper, diced (about ¼ cup)
¼ cup chopped onion
2 small ripe tomatoes, diced and drained
2 cups rotini, cooked and drained
½ cup shredded fat-free Parmesan cheese
  Dressing:
2 tablespoons country Dijon mustard
½ cup bottled white wine vinaigrette dressing
¼ teaspoon crumbled sage

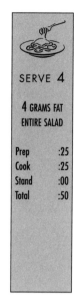

SERVE 4

4 GRAMS FAT
ENTIRE SALAD

Prep	:25
Cook	:25
Stand	:00
Total	:50

In a large mixing bowl, combine the zucchini, mushrooms, lima beans, green pepper, onion, and tomato. Toss lightly to mix. Add the drained pasta and the cheese; toss gently. Set aside.

In a small mixing bowl, combine the dressing ingredients and mix well with a wire whisk. Pour over the salad mixture; gently stir to cover all the ingredients with dressing. May be served at room temperature or chilled.

BOW-TIE PASTA SALAD

SERVES **4**

9 GRAMS FAT
ENTIRE DISH

Prep	:10
Cook	:15
Stand	:30
Total	:55

2 cups bow-tie noodles
1 (14-ounce) can diced tomatoes, drained
1 (4-ounce) can sliced mushrooms, drained
1 (16-ounce) can Great Northern beans, drained and rinsed
½ cup chopped onion
½ cup chopped green pepper
   Dressing:
3 tablespoons bottled white wine vinaigrette with basil and herbs
1 teaspoon bottled Savory Seasonings vegetable oil with roasted
   garlic
Salt and pepper to taste (optional)

Cook the pasta according to package directions, drain, and rinse with cold water. In a medium salad bowl, combine the tomatoes, mushrooms, beans, onion, and pepper. In a small bowl combine the dressing ingredients; mix well with a wire whisk. Pour over the salad, toss gently to evenly coat with dressing. Set aside for about 30 minutes. Serve at room temperature.

QUICK COOL PASTA SALAD

SERVES **4**

1 GRAM FAT
PER SERVING

Prep	:15
Cook	:00
Stand	:30
Total	:45

1½ cups uncooked pasta (preferably lemon-garlic)
1 (15-ounce) can cannellini (white kidney beans), drained and
   rinsed
1 (14-ounce) can small artichoke hearts, drained and quartered
¾ cup chopped green pepper
½ cup chopped onion
1 cup chopped fresh tomato (seeded and drained, then chopped)
2 tablespoons balsamic vinegar

Cook the pasta according to package directions; drain and rinse with cold water. Leave in the colander to drain and cool while you are preparing the salad.

In a large salad bowl, combine all the above ingredients. Add the pasta and toss carefully after adding the vinegar. Let stand about 30 minutes if possible to allow the flavors to marry.

Note: This salad can be made ahead. If you are doing so, do not add the tomato or the vinegar until 30 minutes before serving.

CANNELLINI AND PASTA SALAD

The pasta I used in this salad just happened to be Decio lemon-garlic pasta. If you can't find it, I can tell you just where I got it. Just run up to New York City, go down to Greenwich Village to Balducci's, and there it is. You can use any type, but I thought you might like to know about this particular pasta. (Read the Two Short Blocks to Red Pepper Soup story on pages 13–15.)

SERVES 2

LESS THAN
1 GRAM FAT
PER SERVING

Prep	:10
Cook	:20
Stand	:15
Total	:45

1 cup dry shell-type pasta
1 (16-ounce) can cannellini (white kidney beans), drained and rinsed
1 (14-ounce) can artichoke hearts, drained and chopped
1 Roma tomato, chopped
1 green onion, chopped
1 teaspoon olive oil
¼ cup garlic-flavored red wine vinegar

Cook, drain, and rinse your pasta with cold water according to package directions. In a medium-size mixing bowl, combine the beans, artichoke hearts, tomato, onion, and pasta. Pour the olive oil evenly over, repeat with the vinegar; stir carefully to mix. Let stand about 15 minutes to let the flavors blend.

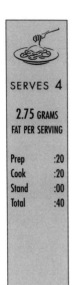

CHICK-PEA AND PASTA SALAD

SERVES 4

2.75 GRAMS
FAT PER SERVING

Prep   :20
Cook   :20
Stand   :00
Total   :40

1 cup dry small shell pasta
1 (15-ounce) can chick-peas, drained
1 cup frozen green peas
½ cup chopped onion
½ cup chopped green pepper
1 cup chopped celery
½ cup finely chopped carrots
    Dressing:
½ cup fat-free Italian salad dressing
2 tablespoons country Dijon mustard
½ teaspoon lemon juice
¼ teaspoon crushed oregano

Cook the pasta according to package directions, drain, and rinse with cold water. Continue draining while assembling the salad.

Combine the chick-peas, green peas (not cooked—straight out of the bag), onion, green pepper, celery, and carrots. Toss lightly. Add the pasta and toss carefully.

In a small bowl, blend all the dressing ingredients with a whisk or fork. Pour the dressing on the salad and stir to mix well. Serve chilled or at room temperature.

THREE-BEAN SALAD

1 (16-ounce) can green beans, drained
1 (16-ounce) can wax beans, drained
1 (15-ounce) can kidney beans, drained and rinsed
4 green onions, with tops, chopped
2 tablespoons snipped parsley
1 cup fat-free Italian dressing
1 teaspoon sugar
1 clove garlic, minced very fine
Lettuce leaves (optional)

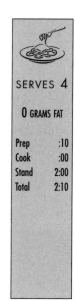

SERVES 6

0 GRAMS FAT

Prep	:10
Cook	:00
Stand	3:00
Total	3:10

In a mixing bowl with a lid, mix the three kinds of beans, the onions, and parsley. In a separate small bowl, mix the Italian dressing, sugar, and garlic. Pour over the bean mixture. Toss to coat evenly. Cover and refrigerate at least 3 hours before serving.

Serve over lettuce leaves, if desired, using a slotted spoon to serve.

CHICK-PEA SALAD

1 cup sliced fresh mushrooms
½ cup chopped green pepper
¼ cup sliced green onions
1 (15-ounce) can chick-peas, drained
½ cup fat-free mayonnaise, such as Miracle Whip
½ cup fat-free Italian dressing
⅛ teaspoon garlic salt
1 teaspoon lemon juice
Lettuce leaves
2 small tomatoes, cut into wedges

SERVES 4

0 GRAMS FAT

Prep	:10
Cook	:00
Stand	2:00
Total	2:10

In a mixing bowl with a lid, combine the mushrooms, green pepper, onions, and chick-peas. Refrigerate until chilled, at least 2 hours.

Make the dressing: In a small bowl, combine the mayonnaise, Italian dressing, garlic salt, and lemon juice. Cover and refrigerate.

Just before serving, toss the salad and dressing together to evenly coat all. Serve on lettuce leaves with tomato wedges to garnish.

THREE-BEAN RICE SALAD

SERVES 6

1 GRAM FAT
PER SERVING

Prep	:15
Cook	:05
Stand	:30
Total	:50

1 (16-ounce) can cut wax beans, drained
1 (16-ounce) can french-style green beans, drained
1 (15-ounce) can cannellini (white kidney beans), drained
¾ cup fat-free Italian salad dressing
1 small onion, minced
Salt and pepper to taste
1½ cups water
1½ cups instant rice
Lettuce leaves (optional)

Mix the drained wax, green, and kidney beans, the salad dressing, onion, salt, and pepper in a large bowl. Set aside to allow the flavors to blend.

Meanwhile bring the water to boil in a medium-size saucepan. Add the rice, cover, remove from the heat, and let stand for about 5 minutes. Uncover, fluff with a fork, and allow to cool.

Combine the rice with the bean mixture, cover, and refrigerate until the rice is chilled. Serve on lettuce if desired.

Sage

This perennial herb, native to the Mediterranean, can grow to a height of about two feet. It is well known for its use in poultry and game stuffing. Its strong flavor demands that it be used with a light touch; mixing parsley and sage can tone down its overpowering flavor. Try it in cheese dishes and spreads, pork recipes, in salads, and cooked in savory breads and soups.

MARINATED MUSHROOMS

1 clove garlic, minced
1 tablespoon olive oil
2 teaspoons dried oregano
1 teaspoon grated lemon peel
Salt and pepper to taste
¼ cup water
1 pound fresh mushrooms, sliced

Combine the garlic, olive oil, oregano, lemon peel, salt, and pepper in a small bowl. Add the ¼ cup of water and whisk until blended.

Place the mushrooms in a glass bowl or a zipper-lock plastic bag; add the dressing and toss gently to mix. Cover and refrigerate for at least 8 hours or overnight. Turn the bag or stir occasionally. Drain the mushrooms before serving. Good served cold or at room temperature.

SERVES 6

3 GRAMS FAT
PER SERVING

Prep	:15
Cook	:00
Stand	8:00
Total	8:15

BABY CARROTS MARINATI

3 cups baby carrots (packaged, already cleaned)
1 small clove garlic, lightly crushed with a heavy knife, peeled
2 tablespoons red wine vinegar
1 teaspoon olive oil
¼ teaspoon dried oregano
Salt and pepper to taste

Place the carrots in saucepan, cover with water, bring to a boil, and cook for about 5 to 6 minutes, just until crisp-tender. (Cooking time varies according to the size of the carrots. The marinade will continue to soften them.)

Drain the carrots and place in a small deep serving dish, not metal. Bury the garlic in the carrots.

In a small dish, combine the vinegar, oil, oregano, salt, and pepper. Pour over the carrots. Cover and refrigerate at least overnight; remove the garlic after 24 hours. Serve at room temperature.

SERVE 4

1.75 GRAMS
FAT PER SERVING

Prep	:15
Cook	:06
Stand	24:00
Total	24:21

SERVES 5

0 GRAMS FAT

Prep   :25
Cook   :30
Stand   :00
Total   :55

HEALTHY POTATO SALAD

Dressing:
1 cup fat-free mayonnaise
¼ teaspoon onion powder
2 tablespoons fat-free Parmesan cheese
½ teaspoon dried oregano
¼ teaspoon sugar
  Salad:
2 cups dried cooked potatoes
1½ cups frozen broccoli cuts, cooked until crisp-tender, drained
2 cups cubed cooked chicken white meat
1 (2-ounce) jar diced pimientos, drained

Make the dressing: In a small mixing bowl, combine the mayonnaise, onion powder, Parmesan, oregano, and sugar. Blend with a wire whisk until smooth.

For the salad: In a medium-size salad bowl, combine the potatoes, broccoli, chicken, and pimiento. Pour the dressing over and toss gently until evenly coated.

SERVES 4

LESS THAN
2 GRAMS FAT
PER SERVING

Prep   :10
Cook   :14
Stand   :35
Total   :59

ANTIPASTO SALAD

1½ cups instant rice (or 3 cups cold cooked rice)
½ to ¾ cup fat-free Italian salad dressing
1 cup diced smoked fat-free sausage, such as Butterball (or any kind of fat-free cooked meat available)
1 cup diced light or fat-free provolone cheese
¼ cup sliced pitted ripe olives
¼ cup roasted red pepper strips

Bring 1½ cups of water to a boil in a medium-size saucepan. Stir in the instant rice, cover, and remove from heat. Let stand until cool.

Put the rice in a serving bowl and pour over ½ cup of Italian dressing, or enough to moisten all the grains. Mix well.

Fold in the smoked sausage, cheese, olives, and pepper strips. Serve at once or cover and chill until serving time.

YOUR CHOICE RICE SALAD

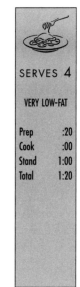

1½ cups instant rice (or 3 cups cold cooked rice)
1¾ cups canned or cooked low-fat meat, seafood, or poultry
1 cup canned or cooked vegetables
½ cup fresh vegetables
¾ cup fat-free mayonnaise
½ cup condiments
Seasoning to taste

SERVES 4

VERY LOW-FAT

Prep	:20
Cook	:00
Stand	1:00
Total	1:20

In a medium-size saucepan, bring 1½ cups of water to a boil, add the instant rice, cover, and let stand about 5 minutes. Fluff with a fork. Cool to room temperature.

Combine meat or seafood and your choice of canned, cooked, and fresh vegetables. Fold in mayonnaise, condiments, and seasonings, blending well. Add the rice and mix gently with a fork. Cover and chill for about an hour.

Suggested Variations:

Meats—Fat-free cold cuts, cut into bite-size pieces; fat-free luncheon meats cut into bite-size pieces
Poultry—Cooked (broiled, baked, boiled) white meat of chicken or turkey, cut into bite-size pieces
Seafood—Tuna, or any seafood you desire. I don't care for seafood, so you will have to use your choice. Watch your fat grams!
Cooked or Canned Vegetables—Artichoke hearts, lima beans, mixed vegetables, peas, peas and carrots, succotash
Fresh Vegetables—Diced celery, mushrooms, green pepper
Seasonings—Capers, chives, garlic, fresh or dried herbs, lemon juice, mustard, onion, parsley
Condiments—Chopped pickles or diced pimientos

SALAD DRESSING

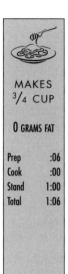

MAKES
³/₄ CUP

0 GRAMS FAT

Prep	:06
Cook	:00
Stand	1:00
Total	1:06

1 clove garlic, crushed
¹/₃ cup water
¹/₈ teaspoon paprika
¹/₄ cup lemon juice
Dash of salt
2 tablespoons honey
1 tablespoon prepared mustard

Combine all ingredients in a container with a lid, such as a jar. Cover tightly and shake until all ingredients are well mixed. Refrigerate at least an hour before serving. Shake well before serving.

CREAMY SALAD DRESSING

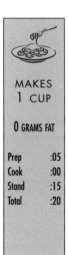

MAKES
1 CUP

0 GRAMS FAT

Prep	:05
Cook	:00
Stand	:15
Total	:20

Very good on fruit salad or green salad.

1 cup fat-free mayonnaise, such as Miracle Whip
1 tablespoon fat-free country Dijon prepared mustard
1 teaspoon skim milk
Pinch of sugar

Combine all ingredients in a mixing bowl and stir with a wire whisk until smooth and creamy. Refrigerate for about 15 minutes to let the flavors blend.

ITALIAN SALAD DRESSING

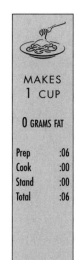

1 cup fat-free French dressing
1 clove garlic, crushed
1 green onion, minced
½ teaspoon dried oregano
Dash of crushed red pepper flakes

MAKES
1 CUP

0 GRAMS FAT

Combine all ingredients in a jar with lid. Shake to combine, and shake again before using.

Prep	:06
Cook	:00
Stand	:00
Total	:06

Note: This is good not only on salads but also poured over boiled or steamed vegetables. You may even pour it over pastas for an excellent quick accent to meals.

VINAIGRETTE SALAD DRESSING

¼ cup red wine vinegar or balsamic vinegar
2 tablespoons orange juice
1 teaspoon sugar
½ teaspoon dry mustard
¼ teaspoon salt
1 teaspoon olive oil
1 green onion, minced

MAKES
½ CUP;
8
SERVINGS

14 GRAMS FAT
ENTIRE RECIPE

Combine all ingredients in a small bowl. Whisk to mix well. Cover and refrigerate for as long as a day ahead. Blend before using.

Prep	:10
Cook	:00
Stand	:00
Total	:10

ROASTED GARLIC

SERVES 6

TRACE OF FAT

Prep :10
Cook :45
Stand :00
Total :55

2 whole heads of garlic

Preheat the oven to 350 degrees.

With a serrated knife, cut off and remove the top third of each garlic head, leaving the roots intact to keep the cloves attached. Place each garlic head on a square of aluminum foil. Spray the garlic lightly with vegetable oil cooking spray and close the foil like a package. Place on a baking dish and bake for 35 to 45 minutes, or until the garlic is soft.

To serve, squeeze the garlic out of the skin and spread on thickly sliced toasted bread or crackers (fat-free of course).

TANGY DIP

MAKES
2¼
CUPS

0 GRAMS FAT

Prep :03
Cook :00
Stand :30
Total :33

2 cups fat-free sour cream
2 tablespoons Dijon mustard
3 green onions, minced
1 teaspoon Worcestershire sauce

In a small bowl combine the sour cream, mustard, minced onions, and Worcestershire. Stir or whisk until well blended. Cover and chill 30 minutes or more before serving.

HERBED DIP

1 cup fat-free sour cream or fat-free cottage cheese
2 tablespoons minced fresh basil or 1 teaspoon crumbled dried basil
1 clove garlic, minced
½ teaspoon grated lemon rind
2 tablespoons chopped red pimientos

Place the sour cream in a small bowl (if you are using cottage cheese, first process it in an electric blender until smooth). Stir in the basil, garlic, lemon rind, and pimiento.

Cover and refrigerate for at least 1 hour before serving.

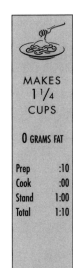

MAKES
1 ¼
CUPS

0 GRAMS FAT

Prep	:10
Cook	:00
Stand	1:00
Total	1:10

CANNELLINI BEAN DIP

2 (15-ounce) cans cannellini beans, drained and rinsed
2 teaspoons finely chopped fresh garlic
1 teaspoon chopped fresh rosemary or ¼ teaspoon dried
⅓ cup fat-free sour cream
Salt and pepper to taste

Place the beans in a microwave-safe bowl and microwave on high for 1 to 2 minutes or until heated through. Set aside.

Spray a nonstick skillet lightly with vegetable oil cooking spray and add the garlic and rosemary. Stir over low heat until the garlic is light golden brown, about 45 seconds. Stir in the sour cream and continue to stir until well blended and heated through (do not allow to boil).

Combine the heated beans and sour cream in the bowl of an electric mixer. Beat at high speed for about 2 minutes, until the beans are whipped but not smooth. Season with salt and pepper to taste.

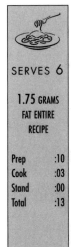

SERVES 6

1.75 GRAMS
FAT ENTIRE
RECIPE

Prep	:10
Cook	:03
Stand	:00
Total	:13

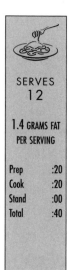

LAYERED PIZZA DIP

SERVES
12

1.4 GRAMS FAT
PER SERVING

Prep	:20
Cook	:20
Stand	:00
Total	:40

1 (8-ounce) package fat-free cream cheese, softened
½ cup fat-free sour cream
¼ teaspoon garlic powder
Dash of ground red pepper (cayenne)
⅔ cup tomato sauce
¼ teaspoon dried oregano
Dash of garlic powder
Dash of onion powder
¼ cup sliced green onions
¼ cup chopped green pepper
¼ cup sliced ripe olives
¾ teaspoon dried Italian seasoning
½ to ¾ cup shredded fat-free mozzarella cheese

Preheat the oven to 350 degrees.

Combine the cream cheese, sour cream, a dash (about ⅛ teaspoon) garlic powder, and the red pepper. Blend with a wire whisk until smooth. Spread the mixture in a 9-inch pie plate sprayed lightly with vegetable oil cooking spray.

Combine the tomato sauce and another dash of garlic powder, the oregano, and the onion powder. Mix well. Pour over the cream cheese mixture. Layer the onions, green pepper, and olives over the tomato sauce. Top with the Italian seasoning and mozzarella.

Bake uncovered for 15 to 20 minutes or until heated through.

Serve warm as a dip with raw vegetables, baked (fat-free) tortilla chips, and/or fat-free crackers.

Pasta

FETTUCCINE

1¼ cups fat-free cottage cheese, at room temperature
½ cup grated fat-free Parmesan cheese
¼ cup minced fresh parsley
Salt and pepper to taste (optional)
8 ounces uncooked fettuccine or other wide noodles (no-egg type)

In a mixing bowl, mash the cottage cheese until smooth. Add the Parmesan cheese, parsley, and salt and pepper if desired. Set aside.

Bring a large pot of salted water to a boil. Add the noodles and cook according to package directions. Drain and return to the same pot.

Pour the cheese sauce over the hot noodles and toss lightly but quickly until the noodles are coated evenly. Serve immediately.

SERVES 4

.5 GRAMS FAT
PER SERVING

Prep	:20
Cook	:00
Stand	:00
Total	:20

FETTUCCINE ALFREDO

SERVES 6

5 GRAMS FAT
PER SERVING

Prep	:25
Cook	:12
Stand	:00
Total	:37

2 cloves garlic, minced
2 tablespoons all-purpose flour
2 tablespoons fat-free cream cheese
1⅓ cups skim milk
2 tablespoons butter sprinkles
1 cup grated fat-free Parmesan cheese
Freshly ground black pepper
8 ounces uncooked fettuccine noodles
1 tablespoon chopped fresh parsley

Spray a medium-size nonstick saucepan or skillet with vegetable oil cooking spray and sauté the garlic until golden, stirring constantly and watching so that it doesn't burn. Remove the pan from the heat and whisk in the flour and cream cheese until well combined. Gradually whisk in the milk, place over medium heat, and bring to a boil while stirring. Remove from the heat again and stir in the butter sprinkles, Parmesan, and black pepper.

Meanwhile, cook the fettuccine in a large pot of boiling salted water until just tender, following package directions. Drain and mix in the sauce, tossing until well combined. Serve garnished with parsley.

SPINACH-STUFFED MANICOTTI I

A recipe for when company comes. The uncooked pasta simmers in the sauce until tender and is enriched with three cheeses.

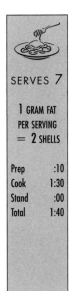

SERVES 7

1 GRAM FAT
PER SERVING
= 2 SHELLS

Prep	:10
Cook	1:30
Stand	:00
Total	1:40

1 (32-ounce) jar low-fat spaghetti sauce, such as Healthy Choice
2 (10-ounce) packages frozen chopped spinach, thawed and squeezed dry
1 (12-ounce) container fat-free cottage cheese
¼ cup grated fat-free Parmesan cheese
1 teaspoon dried oregano leaves
Dash of pepper
14 uncooked manicotti shells
2 cups shredded fat-free mozzarella cheese

Preheat the oven to 350 degrees. Spread about ⅓ cup of the spaghetti sauce in an ungreased 13 x 9 x 2-inch baking dish. Set aside.

In a medium-size bowl, mix the spinach, cottage cheese, Parmesan cheese, oregano, and pepper. Fill the uncooked manicotti shells with the spinach mixture; arrange over the sauce in the baking dish.

Pour the remaining spaghetti sauce evenly over the shells, making sure to cover each one. Sprinkle with mozzarella cheese. Cover with foil and bake for about 1½ hours or until the shells are tender.

SPINACH-STUFFED MANICOTTI II

A quicker version for a busy day, this recipe uses cooked pasta shells.

SERVES 4

1 GRAM FAT
PER SERVING

Prep   :15
Cook   :45
Stand   :00
Total   1:00

1 (8-ounce) box manicotti shells
1 (16-ounce) container light ricotta cheese
1 (10-ounce) package frozen spinach, cooked, squeezed dry, and chopped
1/4 teaspoon Italian seasoning
Prepared low-fat spaghetti sauce

Preheat the oven to 350 degrees. Lightly spray a 13 x 9 x 2-inch baking dish with vegetable oil cooking spray.

Cook and drain the pasta shells according to package directions. Set aside. Mix the ricotta, spinach, and Italian seasoning. Stuff the shells with the mixture. Arrange in the baking dish. Pour spaghetti sauce over and bake uncovered for 25 to 30 minutes or until hot and bubbly.

VEGETABLE LASAGNE

3 1/3 cups low-fat spaghetti sauce
1 medium zucchini, shredded
6 uncooked lasagne noodles
1 cup light ricotta or small-curd fat-free cottage cheese
1/4 cup grated fat-free Parmesan cheese
3/4 teaspoon dried oregano leaves
2 cups shredded fat-free mozzarella cheese

SERVES 6

VERY LOW-FAT

Prep	:10
Cook	:50
Stand	:15
Total	1:15

Preheat the oven to 350 degrees.

Mix the spaghetti sauce and zucchini. Spread about 1 cup of the sauce mixture in an ungreased 11 x 7-inch baking dish. Top with 3 of the uncooked noodles.

Mix the ricotta, Parmesan cheese, and oregano; spread over the noodles in the baking dish. Spread with about 1 cup of the sauce mixture.

Place the remaining noodles over these layers; top with another layer of the sauce mixture and the mozzarella cheese. Bake uncovered for 45 to 50 minutes or until bubbly. Let stand 15 minutes before serving.

ZUCCHINI LASAGNE

SERVES 6

LESS THAN
2 GRAMS FAT
PER SERVING

Prep   :35
Cook   1:20
Stand   :15
Total   2:10

1 cup chopped onion
1 cup chopped green pepper
1 (16-ounce) can tomatoes, undrained
3 tablespoons tomato paste or pasta sauce
Salt and pepper to taste
1 teaspoon sugar
18 no-boil lasagne noodles
2 medium zucchini, chopped
1 cup finely chopped summer (yellow) squash
1 (16-ounce) package fat-free mozzarella cheese, shredded (about
    2 cups)

In a large nonstick skillet, sauté the onion and pepper in ¼ cup of water until just crisp-tender. Add the tomatoes, liquid and all, tomato paste or pasta sauce, salt and pepper, sugar, and 2½ cups of water. Heat to boil. Reduce heat and simmer 15 minutes over medium low heat. Stir the sauce occasionally.

Preheat the oven to 350 degrees. Spread ⅓ of the sauce evenly over the bottom of a 13 x 9 x 2-inch baking dish that has been lightly sprayed with vegetable oil cooking spray. Arrange half the noodles in a single layer, overlapping as necessary to fit in the baking dish. (These are no-boil noodles; just put them in the pan, dry and hard.) Top with the chopped zucchini and yellow squash. Sprinkle with 1 cup of the cheese and half the remaining sauce. Layer the rest of the noodles, the remaining sauce, and the remaining 1 cup cheese.

Cover the dish tightly with aluminum foil and bake 40 to 50 minutes. Uncover and bake 15 more minutes. Let stand 15 minutes before cutting to serve.

MACARONI AND CHEESE

1 cup fine dry unflavored bread crumbs
2 cups fat-free ricotta cheese
1½ cups skim milk
1 tablespoon all-purpose flour
8 ounces (about 2 cups) dried elbow macaroni
1½ cups fat-free mozzarella cheese, cut into chunks
Salt and pepper to taste (optional)

SERVES 4

4 GRAMS FAT
ENTIRE DISH

Prep	:15
Cook	1:00
Stand	:05
Total	1:20

In a nonstick skillet lightly sprayed with vegetable oil cooking spray, brown the bread crumbs, spraying and stirring them until nice and brown, 8 to 10 minutes. Set aside.

Combine the ricotta cheese and ½ cup of the milk in a blender or food processor. Process until smooth; set aside. In a small bowl, whisk the flour and ¼ cup of the milk together until smooth; set aside.

Bring 8 cups of water to a boil in a large saucepan. Stir in the macaroni and cook 8 to 10 minutes or just until tender. Meanwhile, heat the remaining ¾ cup of milk in a medium saucepan until steaming—do not boil. Add the flour mixture, whisking until smooth. Cook, stirring often, until the mixture begins to thicken, about 2 or 3 minutes. Remove from the heat and stir in the ricotta cheese mixture and the mozzarella. Stir until the cheese is melted.

Preheat the oven to 350 degrees.

Drain the pasta well. Add it to the cheese mixture and mix thoroughly but gently. Season to taste with salt and pepper if desired. Transfer to a 2½-quart casserole that has been lightly coated with cooking spray. Cover tightly with foil and bake for 25 minutes. Uncover, sprinkle the bread crumbs over the top, and continue to bake until top is lightly browned and the mixture is bubbling. Let stand about 5 minutes before serving.

LASAGNE ROLL-UPS

SERVES **4**

3 GRAMS FAT
PER SERVING

Prep	:30
Cook	1:00
Stand	:00
Total	1:30

1 large yellow onion, chopped fine
1 teaspoon crumbled dried basil
½ teaspoon crumbled dried marjoram
1 bay leaf, crumbled
¾ teaspoon black pepper
2 cloves garlic, minced
1 skinless boneless chicken breast, chopped fine
1 (16-ounce) can tomatoes, chopped, with their juice
2 tablespoons tomato paste
8 ruffle-edge lasagne noodles
½ cup grated fat-free Parmesan cheese
1 cup fat-free cottage cheese or part-skim ricotta cheese
1 (10-ounce) package frozen chopped spinach, thawed and
   squeezed dry
¼ teaspoon grated nutmeg
¼ teaspoon cream of tartar

In a nonstick skillet lightly sprayed with olive oil cooking spray, sauté the onion, basil, marjoram, bay leaf, and ¼ teaspoon of the pepper.

Cook over medium heat, stirring, for 4 minutes. Add half the garlic and cook for 1 more minute. Remove about 2 tablespoons of the mixture from the skillet and set aside.

Add the chopped chicken to the skillet and cook, stirring, for 3 to 4 minutes. Reduce the heat to low, add the tomatoes and tomato paste, and cook for 20 minutes, stirring occasionally. Set the sauce aside.

Meanwhile, cook the lasagne noodles according to package directions, omitting the salt. Rinse with cold water and drain.

Preheat the oven to 375 degrees. To make the filling for the lasagne noodles, combine 5 tablespoons of the Parmesan cheese in a medium-size bowl with the cottage cheese, spinach, nutmeg, cream of tartar, and the remaining garlic and pepper. Add the reserved onion mixture. Mix well.

Spoon half the sauce into an ungreased 9 x 9-inch baking dish.

Spread 3 tablespoons of the cheese filling on each lasagne noodle and roll up into a tight coil. Place seam side down in the pan, repeating until all noodles are rolled. Top with the remaining sauce.

Cover with aluminum foil and bake for 25 minutes. Uncover, sprinkle the remaining Parmesan cheese on top, and bake uncovered for 5 minutes longer.

LINGUINE

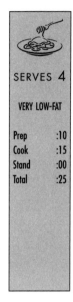

2 slices turkey bacon, coarsely chopped
1½ cups skim milk
½ cup chopped red bell pepper (may substitute green)
¼ teaspoon crushed red pepper flakes
1 tablespoon cornstarch
¼ cup egg substitute
½ cup frozen green peas, thawed
8 ounces dried linguine (or spaghetti), cooked and drained
¼ cup shredded low-fat Parmesan cheese (1 ounce)
Freshly ground black pepper
Freshly grated low-fat Parmesan cheese (optional)

SERVES 4

VERY LOW-FAT

Prep	:10
Cook	:15
Stand	:00
Total	:25

In a deep nonstick skillet or saucepan, cook the bacon until crisp. Drain on a paper towel and wipe the pan clean with paper towels.

For the sauce: In the same pan, combine the milk, red bell pepper, and pepper flakes. Bring to a boil, lower the heat, and simmer for about 2 more minutes. In a small bowl, dissolve the cornstarch in 2 tablespoons of cold water. Stir into the milk mixture, add the egg substitute, and continue stirring until thick and bubbly, 30 to 40 seconds longer. Stir in the peas and bacon. Heat through.

Immediately pour the sauce over the hot cooked linguine or spaghetti; toss to coat. Serve on heated plates, sprinkled with the Parmesan cheese and black pepper. Additional Parmesan may be passed if desired.

VEGETABLE AND PASTA ALL-DAY STEW

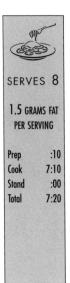

SERVES 8

1.5 GRAMS FAT
PER SERVING

Prep	:10
Cook	7:10
Stand	:00
Total	7:20

This is a great dish for the working person to put on before leaving for work in the morning and finish when returning in the evening. You may want to set your cooker on medium heat if leaving for a full 8 or 9 hours. Then turn to high when you return and continue the recipe.

2 cups chopped onion
1¾ cups small red potatoes, scrubbed and quartered
1 cup dried Great Northern beans
½ cup sliced carrots
¾ cup quartered fresh mushrooms
½ cup pearl barley (optional)
½ pound boneless, skinless chicken white meat, cut into large chunks
1 (14-ounce) can pasta-style chunky tomatoes, juice and all
1 (14-ounce) can fat-free chicken broth
3 cloves garlic, chopped
1 cup sliced zucchini
1 cup chopped fresh spinach leaves
1 cup small pasta, such as alphabets or stars
1 tablespoon dried rosemary, crushed
1 teaspoon salt
½ teaspoon ground black pepper
1 teaspoon rubbed sage
¼ teaspoon grated nutmeg
½ cup fat-free Parmesan cheese (optional)

In a large Crock-Pot or electric cooker, combine 5 cups of water, the onion, potatoes, dried beans, carrots, mushrooms, barley, chicken, tomatoes, chicken broth, and garlic. Cover and cook on high heat for a minimum of 6½ hours.

Stir in the zucchini, spinach, pasta, rosemary, salt, pepper, sage, and nutmeg. Cover and cook on high heat for an additional 30 to 40 minutes.

Check to see if the beans are tender after this additional cooking time. If not, continue to cook until they are done. Serve the stew in individual soup bowls. Sprinkle with cheese (fat-free of course) if desired.

SPAGHETTI WITH GARDEN VEGETABLE SAUCE

A quick healthy dinner. I sure do miss Dad's garden and all the wonderful veggies, but my brother fills in pretty good.

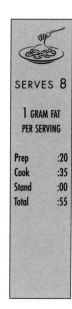

SERVES 8

1 GRAM FAT
PER SERVING

Prep	:20
Cook	:35
Stand	:00
Total	:55

2 small onions, peeled and cut into eighths
3 ripe tomatoes, peeled and cut into eighths
1 small yellow summer squash, sliced thin
1 small zucchini squash, sliced thin
1 cup sliced fresh green beans
1 tablespoon minced fresh parsley
1 clove garlic, minced
½ teaspoon Italian seasoning
¼ teaspoon salt
Dash of pepper
1 (6-ounce) can tomato paste
1 (16-ounce) package uncooked spaghetti
½ cup grated fat-free Parmesan cheese

In a large saucepan, nonstick if available, combine the onions, tomatoes, both squash, green beans, ¾ cup of water, the parsley, garlic, Italian seasoning, salt, and pepper. Cook uncovered for 10 minutes, then stir in the tomato paste. Cover and cook over very low heat for an additional 15 minutes, stirring occasionally, until vegetables are tender.

Meanwhile, bring a large pot of water to boil and cook the spaghetti according to package directions (omitting salt). Drain the spaghetti, and spoon the vegetable sauce over, either on individual plates or a large serving plate. Sprinkle the Parmesan cheese over the top.

CAPELLINI AND CANNELLINI

SERVES 4

1 GRAM FAT
PER SERVING

Prep	:15
Cook	1:15
Stand	:00
Total	1:30

1 cup (1½-inch) red onion chunks
6 tablespoons balsamic vinegar
12 medium-size Roma tomatoes, halved lengthwise
Salt and pepper to taste
2 cups dried capellini pasta
2 (15-ounce) cans cannellini (white kidney beans), undrained
1 tablespoon dried thyme
1 tablespoon dried basil

Preheat the oven to 450 degrees. Heavily spray an 8-inch baking pan with olive oil cooking spray. Mix the onion and 2 tablespoons of the vinegar in the sprayed pan and roll the pan around to mix the sprayed oil and vinegar with the onion. Arrange the tomatoes cut sides up in a lightly sprayed 13 x 9-inch baking pan; spray tomatoes lightly with cooking spray. Season to taste with salt and pepper.

Place both pans in the oven and bake, switching pan positions halfway through baking, until the edges are well browned (40 to 50 minutes for the onion, and about 1 hour and 10 minutes for the tomatoes). If the vegetables begin to burn, add 5 or 6 tablespoons of water to each pan.

Meanwhile, bring a large pot of water to a boil and cook the capellini according to package directions just until tender to the bite. Drain and keep warm.

Pour the beans, liquid and all, into a large saucepan; add the thyme and basil. Bring to a boil, reduce the heat, and simmer, stirring often, for about 3 minutes. Add the pasta, lifting with pasta forks or servers to mix. Remove from the heat and keep warm.

Chop the roasted tomato halves; add the pasta, along with the onion and the remaining ¼ cup of vinegar. Toss to mix. Pour into wide shallow pasta bowl; serve immediately.

Note: If you are in a hurry and can't spend 1½ hours roasting these tomatoes and onions, do what I do when I am in a hurry, which is about 99 percent of the time: Spray a nonstick skillet with the olive oil cooking spray and sauté the tomatoes and onions until the onions are lightly browned. Pour into a holding dish while you continue the recipe as above.

SPAGHETTI PIE

6 ounces uncooked spaghetti
3 tablespoons fat-free liquid-type margarine
1 tablespoon egg substitute
½ cup grated fat-free Parmesan cheese
1 pound low-fat turkey sausage
½ cup chopped onion
¼ cup chopped green pepper
1 (8-ounce) can tomatoes, cut up, with their juice
1 (6-ounce) can tomato paste
1 teaspoon sugar
1 teaspoon oregano
Dash of garlic salt
1 cup fat-free ricotta cheese, drained
½ cup shredded fat-free mozzarella cheese

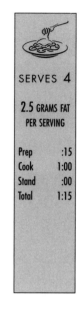

SERVES 4

2.5 GRAMS FAT
PER SERVING

Prep	:15
Cook	1:00
Stand	:00
Total	1:15

Preheat the oven to 350 degrees.

Bring a large pot of water to a boil and cook the spaghetti according to package directions. Drain and return to the pan. Stir in the margarine, egg substitute, and Parmesan cheese. Press the spaghetti into a pie plate that has been sprayed with vegetable oil cooking oil spray, forming a crust. Set aside.

In a nonstick skillet, cook the turkey sausage with the onion and green pepper, stirring to break apart the sausage, until brown. Drain, place in a colander, rinse with the hottest water in your tap, and shake off excess water. Place in a saucepan; stir in the tomatoes, tomato paste, sugar, oregano, and garlic salt. Heat thoroughly. Spread the ricotta over the bottom of the spaghetti crust. Top with the meat mixture.

Bake uncovered for 20 minutes. Sprinkle with mozzarella and bake 5 minutes more, or until the cheese is melted.

MOCK PASTA ALFREDO

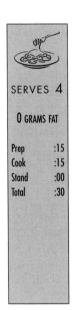

SERVES 4

0 GRAMS FAT

Prep	:15
Cook	:15
Stand	:00
Total	:30

1½ cups fat-free cottage cheese or ricotta cheese
½ cup skim milk (0 grams fat—read label)
2 cloves garlic, minced
2 tablespoons all-purpose flour
1 tablespoon lemon juice
1 teaspoon dried basil
¼ teaspoon dry mustard
¼ teaspoon pepper
Dash of salt (optional)
8 ounces pasta of your choice, cooked and drained
Fresh tomatoes, seeded and chopped, if desired, for garnish

In a blender or food processor, process the cottage cheese, milk, and garlic, until smooth. Add the flour, lemon juice, basil, mustard, pepper, and salt if desired. Process until well blended.

Pour into a heavy saucepan and cook over medium heat until thickened. *Do not boil.* Serve hot over pasta of your choice. Sprinkle with chopped tomatoes if desired.

Parsley

Originating in the Mediterranean countries, parsley was one of the first greens to be used for making wreaths. It has been thought to increase virility in males and fertility in females, and has been given credit for curing a host of ailments.
Hard to grow, on account of its long germination period, parsley prefers moist soil and a partially shaded area.
Parsley is perhaps the most nutrient-rich of all the herbs. It's an excellent source of vitamins A, B, and C, as well as iron and calcium.
Use it in soups, stews, or salads. Almost any dish is nice with parsley except sweets. The most popular garnish known, it is even said to sweeten your breath.

PASTA PRIMAVERA

1 (8-ounce) package spaghetti, fettuccine, or other pasta
1 clove garlic, minced
1 medium-size red bell pepper, seeded and sliced small
½ pound snow peas, trimmed
3 cups broccoli florets
1 cup diced green onions
¼ cup chopped parsley
1 tablespoon crumbled dried basil leaves
Freshly ground pepper to taste
¼ cup fat-free Parmesan cheese

SERVES 4

2 GRAMS FAT
PER SERVING

Prep	:15
Cook	:10
Stand	:00
Total	:25

Prepare the pasta according to package directions. Drain.

Spray a large nonstick skillet lightly with olive oil cooking spray. Place over medium-high heat; add garlic, bell pepper, snow peas, broccoli, onions, and parsley. Cook 1 minute, stirring constantly. Cover and cook 4 to 5 minutes longer, stirring occasionally.

Add the basil and cooked pasta to the vegetable mixture; toss well until the pasta is heated. Turn onto a serving platter and sprinkle with pepper and Parmesan cheese.

SPAGHETTI WITH RICOTTA PESTO

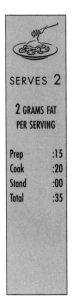

SERVES 2

2 GRAMS FAT
PER SERVING

Prep	:15
Cook	:20
Stand	:00
Total	:35

1 (10-ounce) package frozen chopped spinach, thawed and
squeezed dry
½ cup hot water
⅓ cup fat-free ricotta cheese (may substitute cottage cheese)
⅓ cup snipped fresh basil or 2 tablespoons crushed dried basil
2 tablespoons grated fat-free Parmesan cheese
2 tablespoons olive oil
2 cloves garlic, minced
4 ounces uncooked spaghetti

In a blender container or food processor bowl, combine the
spinach, water, ricotta, basil, Parmesan cheese, oil, and garlic.
Blend or process until smooth. Set the pesto aside.

Bring a large pot of water to a boil. Add the pasta and cook
according to package directions until tender but still firm. Drain.

Spoon half the pesto over the hot, cooked pasta; toss to mix
well. Serve immediately.

ANGEL HAIR WITH GREMOLATA

*Angel hair pasta, which is very fine, must be served
immediately after it's cooked.*

16 ounces angel hair pasta
1 tablespoon extra-light olive oil
1 recipe Gremolata (page 177)
½ teaspoon salt
Dash of pepper
5 tablespoons grated fat-free Parmesan cheese (see Note)

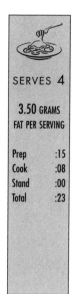

SERVES 4

3.50 GRAMS
FAT PER SERVING

Prep	:15
Cook	:08
Stand	:00
Total	:23

Bring a large pot of water to a boil. Add the pasta and cook for
2 to 3 minutes or until tender but still firm. Drain and keep hot.

Warm the olive oil in a large nonstick skillet. Add the gremolata,
salt, and pepper. Cook and stir for no longer than 1 minute—take
care that the garlic doesn't burn! Add the drained pasta, salt,
pepper, and Parmesan. Toss to combine; serve right away.

Note: Fresh Parmesan grated fine is even better, but be careful of fat grams.

BAKED ZITI ITALIAN STYLE

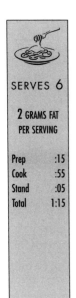

SERVES 6

**2 GRAMS FAT
PER SERVING**

Prep	:15
Cook	:55
Stand	:05
Total	1:15

1 (16-ounce) package ziti, rigatoni, or other tube-shaped pasta
1 large onion, chopped
2 medium zucchini, trimmed and diced
3 garlic cloves, minced
1 (28-ounce) can tomatoes crushed in purée
2 teaspoons dried Italian seasoning
1/4 teaspoon crushed red pepper flakes
Salt and pepper to taste
1/2 cup egg substitute
1 (15-ounce) container fat-free ricotta cheese
2/3 cup shredded fat-free mozzarella cheese
1/2 cup grated fat-free Parmesan cheese

Bring a large pot of water to a boil, add the ziti, and cook 10 to 12 minutes, or until tender but still firm. Drain and set aside.

Preheat the oven to 325 degrees. Lightly coat a 13 x 9 x 2-inch baking dish with vegetable oil cooking spray.

In a large nonstick pan, over medium heat, sauté the onion, zucchini, and garlic, stirring constantly, for about 1 minute. Stir in the tomatoes and their purée, the Italian seasoning, and pepper flakes. Cover and cook about 10 minutes, or until the vegetables are very soft. Season with salt and pepper to taste.

In a small bowl blend together the egg substitute and ricotta cheese until smooth.

Place the drained pasta in an even layer in the prepared baking dish. Cover with a layer of the ricotta cheese and top with the tomato mixture. Sprinkle with the mozzarella and Parmesan.

Bake uncovered for about 45 minutes or until golden brown on top and bubbling. Let stand 5 minutes before cutting and serving.

SPAGHETTI WITH CHICKEN AND BROCCOLI

Serve this as soon as possible after cooking.
Spaghetti waits for no one.

2 bunches broccoli
1 teaspoon olive oil
8 boneless skinless chicken tenders
3/4 cup chopped onion
1 clove garlic, minced
1 cup dry white wine
1 (16-ounce) package spaghetti

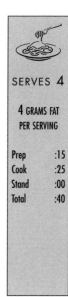

SERVES 4

4 GRAMS FAT
PER SERVING

Prep	:15
Cook	:25
Stand	:00
Total	:40

Separate the broccoli florets from the stalks, reserving the stalks for another purpose. Cut the florets apart into approximately 1-inch lengths. Bring a large pot of water to a boil, drop in the florets, and cook just until crisp-tender, about 4 to 5 minutes. Remove with a slotted spoon and drop the florets into a bowl of ice water to stop from further cooking. Drain. (Reserve the pot of water for cooking the spaghetti.)

In a large nonstick skillet, heat the olive oil and brown the chicken on both sides. Push to the side of the pan and add the onion and garlic. Sauté until the onion is very soft. You don't want to pull the flavor from the broccoli by having your onion too strong —the softer it is, the milder the flavor. When the onion is cooked, add the wine and simmer for 2 or 3 minutes, scraping up the browned bits from the bottom of the pan. Add the broccoli and stir until heated through.

Meanwhile, return the pot of water to a boil and add the spaghetti. Cook for 10 to 12 minutes or until tender but still firm. Drain. Combine the spaghetti with the chicken and broccoli, stirring until mixed. Serve at once.

SPAGHETTI LASAGNE

SERVES 6

2 GRAMS FAT PER SERVING

Prep   :35
Cook   :55
Stand   :10
Total   1:40

6 ounces dry spaghetti (about ½ package)
1 (26-ounce) jar super-chunky vegetable pasta primavera sauce, such as Healthy Choice
1 small eggplant
Salt
1 cup chopped onion
¾ cup chopped green bell pepper
2 cloves garlic, minced
1 teaspoon mild Italian pizza seasoning
2 cups cooked chicken breast cut into short thin strips
3 to 4 tablespoons fat-free ricotta cheese (or substitute fat-free cottage cheese)
½ cup shredded fat-free mozzarella cheese
2 teaspoons fat-free Parmesan cheese
⅛ teaspoon crushed red pepper flakes
2 teaspoons Italian-style bread crumbs

Preheat the oven to 350 degrees. Spray an 8 x 12-inch baking dish with olive oil cooking spray. Set aside.

Bring a large pot of water to a boil, add the spaghetti, and cook for 10 to 12 minutes or until tender but still firm. Drain. You should have about 3 cups of cooked pasta.

Place the cooked, drained spaghetti and about ¾ cup of the pasta sauce in a medium bowl. Stir to coat evenly. Pour into the prepared baking dish. Move the spaghetti around to form a crust appearance, pushing up the sides a little and leaving the crust thinner on the bottom. Bake for about 10 minutes. Remove from heat and set aside.

While the crust is baking, peel the eggplant, cube, and cover with salt water, about 2 quarts of water and 2 tablespoons of salt.

Meanwhile, heat ¼ cup of water in a nonstick skillet and sauté the onion, green pepper, garlic, and Italian seasoning. Drain the eggplant and add to the skillet. Continue to cook, stirring occasionally. When the vegetables are just crisp-tender, add the chicken and stir until the chicken is heated. Turn the heat off.

With a fork, spread the ricotta cheese as evenly as possible over the bottom of the crust. Cover with the chicken and vegetable mixture and top with the remaining pasta sauce, spreading only to the spaghetti crust, not to the edge of the baking dish. Sprinkle mozzarella cheese over the sauce, then sprinkle the Parmesan over evenly, the crushed pepper next, and the bread crumbs sprinkled over all.

Bake uncovered for 45 to 50 minutes or until hot and bubbly. Let stand about 10 minutes before serving.

Variation:

You may want to add a layer of chopped black olives and/or mushrooms. Use your imagination, but remember that the olives will add fat grams, as will any other addition with fat. This is a great dish for little leftover portions of vegetables. I don't throw anything away.

LIGHT & LEAN DINNER FOR TWO

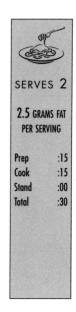

6 boneless skinless chicken tenders
1 small onion, chopped (about ¾ cup)
½ teaspoon chopped garlic
1 teaspoon chopped fresh parsley
½ cup red wine
1 (14½-ounce) can stewed tomatoes, Italian style, drained and chopped
1 cup frozen green peas
1 cup bow-tie pasta, cooked according to package directions
1 teaspoon Parmesan grated cheese

SERVES 2

2.5 GRAMS FAT
PER SERVING

Prep	:15
Cook	:15
Stand	:00
Total	:30

Brown the chicken in a nonstick skillet. When browned and tender, add the onion and continue to sauté for about 2 minutes. Stir in the garlic. Add the parsley and stir in well. Pour in the wine; simmer for 3 to 4 minutes. Add the tomatoes, peas, and cooked pasta and stir in well. Simmer for 4 to 5 minutes. Sprinkle cheese over all; toss to mix. Spoon onto serving dishes.

CHICKEN, VEGETABLES, AND LINGUINE WITH WHITE SAUCE

SERVES 4

4 FAT GRAMS PER SERVING

Prep	:15
Cook	:45
Stand	:00
Total	1:00

4 boneless skinless chicken breast halves
6 ounces uncooked linguine
2¼ cups skim milk, or as needed
2 tablespoons cornstarch
2 cups fresh vegetables, cut up (yellow squash, green peas, asparagus, broccoli, zucchini, carrots, your choice) (see Note)
Salt and pepper to taste

Place the chicken in a large saucepan, add water to just cover, and bring to a boil. Lower the heat and cook until tender, about 20 to 30 minutes. Remove the chicken from the broth with a slotted spoon. Defat the broth: Cool and spoon off the fat that rises to the top, or use a defatting pitcher with a low spout—you pour your broth from the bottom and the fat stays on top.

Return the broth to the saucepan and bring back up to a boil. Add the linguine and boil until tender but still firm, about 8 minutes. Drain in a colander. (You may reserve the broth for another dish another day. You can always add flavor by using chicken stock instead of water in some dishes.)

Return the linguine to the saucepan, cover with 2 cups of milk, and turn the heat to medium.

In a cup, mix 2 tablespoons of cornstarch with the remaining ¼ cup of cold milk. When the linguine and milk are near boiling, add the cornstarch while stirring. Add the chicken and vegetables. Remove from the heat when the sauce reaches the desired thickness. Season to taste.

Note: You may steam vegetables ahead of time if desired or use leftover veggies. I use mine raw—we like crisp tender vegetables.

OKRAHOMA ITALIAN CHICKEN, PASTA, AND VEGETABLES

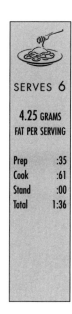

20 to 24 large pasta shells (suitable for stuffing)
1 (15-ounce) container light ricotta cheese
1 teaspoon Italian seasoning
1 (10-ounce) package frozen chopped spinach, cooked and squeezed dry
2 boneless skinless chicken breast halves
½ cup chopped onion
½ teaspoon chopped garlic
1 cup diced yellow summer squash
½ pound okra pods, cut in 1-inch pieces, cooked, and drained (about 2 cups)
1 cup prepared low-fat pasta sauce
1 cup tomato sauce

SERVES 6

4.25 GRAMS
FAT PER SERVING

Prep	:35
Cook	:61
Stand	:00
Total	1:36

Preheat the oven to 350 degrees. Lightly coat an 8 x 12-inch baking dish with vegetable oil cooking spray.

Bring a large saucepan of water to a boil and cook the pasta shells about 10 minutes. Do not overcook. Drain and rinse with cold water; drain again.

In a small bowl, mix the ricotta cheese, Italian seasoning, and spinach. Stuff each shell with some of the mixture and arrange in the prepared dish. Set aside.

Heat a nonstick skillet and brown the chicken breasts on both sides. While the chicken cooks, place the chopped onion around the edge of the skillet and cook, stirring often, for about 5 minutes. Add the garlic and cook for 1 minute longer. Don't let your garlic burn! When the chicken is browned, cut into small chunks and distribute them evenly over the pasta shells. Stir the squash into the onions and spread over the chicken. Dot with the okra. Mix the pasta sauce and tomato sauce and pour over all. Bake uncovered for 40 to 45 minutes.

Variation:

For a simplified version, omit the chicken and vegetables. Just prepare pasta shells with the stuffing, pour the combined sauces over, and bake for only about 15 minutes.

LITTLE ITALY

SERVES 6

4 FAT GRAMS
PER SERVING

Prep	:10
Cook	:35
Stand	:00
Total	:45

6 to 8 boneless skinless chicken tenders
1 small onion, chopped (about ½ cup)
1 small green pepper, chopped (about ½ cup)
¾ cup shredded Canadian bacon or thinly sliced ham
1 teaspoon minced garlic
1 (16-ounce) can stewed tomatoes
1½ cups frozen green peas
1½ cups eggless noodles or macaroni
Salt and pepper to taste

Brown the chicken on both sides in a nonstick skillet. Add the onion, green pepper, Canadian bacon, and garlic. Sauté for 5 to 6 minutes, stirring to let the onion, pepper, and bacon cook evenly.

Add the tomatoes and peas. Simmer for 10 to 12 minutes, stirring occasionally. Meantime, cook the noodles or macaroni (spiral macaroni is nice) in a large pot of boiling water until tender but still firm. Drain, add to the chicken and sauce, and continue to simmer about 10 minutes more. Add salt and pepper if desired.

LINGUINE WITH CHICKEN

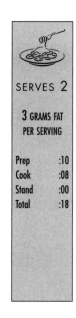

½ cup chopped onion
¾ cup chopped green pepper
1 teaspoon minced garlic
1½ cups cubed cooked chicken
1½ cups tomato sauce, or your favorite prepared marinara sauce (see Note)
8 ounces linguine, cooked according to package directions
2 tablespoons fat-free Parmesan cheese

SERVES 2

3 GRAMS FAT
PER SERVING

Prep	:10
Cook	:08
Stand	:00
Total	:18

In a nonstick skillet, bring ¼ cup water to a boil and sauté the onion, pepper, and garlic for 3 minutes or until they are crisp-tender and about half done. Add the chicken and cook until heated. Add the sauce and stir until heated. Be careful to lower your heat or it will bubble and splatter.

Pour the sauce over the hot cooked linguine and top with Parmesan cheese. (Use fresh Parmesan if it's available, but be careful to count the grams you're adding.)

Note: Be careful—read your label for fat grams. You may even use a prepared spaghetti sauce if it's healthy and low-fat.

ROSEMARY CHICKEN AND SPAGHETTI

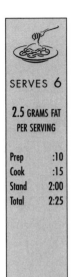

SERVES 6

2.5 GRAMS FAT
PER SERVING

Prep	:10
Cook	:15
Stand	2:00
Total	2:25

12 chicken tenders (or any white-meat pieces) (see Note)
½ cup white wine vinegar
2 tablespoons chopped fresh rosemary leaves or 2 teaspoons dried
1 teaspoon grated lemon peel
¾ teaspoon crushed red pepper flakes
2 to 3 tomatoes, peeled and chopped (about 1 cup)
1 teaspoon toasted pine nuts
1 (16-ounce) package spaghetti or other pasta

Cut the chicken into strips about ½ inch wide and 2 inches long.

In a shallow nonreactive baking dish, combine the vinegar, rosemary, and lemon peel. Add the chicken, cover, and marinate in the refrigerator for at least 2 hours.

Place a large nonstick skillet over medium-high heat and spray with olive oil cooking spray. Sauté the crushed red pepper for 1 minute; just before it starts to smoke, add the chicken and its marinade. Cook for 2 minutes, or until the chicken is lightly browned, stirring constantly. Add the tomatoes and pine nuts. Cook about ½ minute longer, stirring constantly. Reduce the heat to low; cover and simmer 10 minutes, or until the tomatoes are soft.

Meanwhile, bring a large pot of water to a boil. Add the pasta and cook according to package directions until tender but still firm. Drain.

Mix the hot drained spaghetti with the sauce; toss to combine. Serve on a warm platter.

Note: I use tenders because they only have .5 grams fat each and are frozen and ready at all times.

CHICKEN AND RIGATONI

2 cups uncooked rigatoni
8 boneless skinless chicken tenders
½ cup chopped onion
¼ cup chopped green pepper
2 (10¾-ounce) cans pasta-style tomatoes
1 (4-ounce) can V-8 juice
¾ cup water
½ teaspoon dried basil
½ teaspoon dried oregano
Salt and pepper to taste

SERVES 4

2 GRAMS FAT
PER SERVING

Prep	:10
Cook	:30
Stand	:00
Total	:40

Cook the rigatoni according to package directions, omitting any oil or salt. Drain but do not rinse. Set aside.

Sauté the chicken tenders, onion, and green pepper in a large nonstick skillet, cooking until lightly browned.

Add the tomatoes, V-8 juice, water, and pasta. Stir in the seasonings and simmer until well blended. Serve hot.

BAKED SPAGHETTI

SERVES
12

VERY LOW-FAT
(ABOUT
3 GRAMS
PER SERVING)

Prep	:35
Cook	:45
Stand	:10
Total	1:30

1 pound fat-free ground turkey
1 cup chopped onion
1 cup chopped green pepper
¼ cup water
1 (28-ounce) can tomatoes, cut up, with liquid
1 (4-ounce) can mushroom stems and pieces, drained
½ cup sliced ripe olives, drained
2 teaspoons dried oregano
12 ounces spaghetti, cooked according to package directions
2 cups shredded fat-free cheese (your choice)
1 (10¾-ounce) can Healthy Choice cream of mushroom soup,
   undiluted, and ½ soup can water
¼ cup grated fat-free Parmesan cheese

Preheat the oven to 350 degrees. Lightly coat a 13 x 9 x 2-inch baking dish with vegetable oil cooking spray.

In a large nonstick skillet, dry-fry the ground turkey over medium heat, stirring to break up lumps, until the meat starts to brown. Place the turkey in a colander and rinse with hot water to remove all traces of fat. Drain well.

In the same skillet, sauté the onion and green pepper in ¼ cup water for 5 minutes or until tender. Add the tomatoes, mushrooms, olives, and oregano. Stir in the turkey. Simmer uncovered for 10 minutes.

Place half the hot cooked spaghetti in the prepared baking dish. Top with half the turkey-vegetable mixture and sprinkle with 1 cup of the shredded cheese. Repeat the layers. Mix the soup and ½ cup water until smooth; pour over the casserole. Sprinkle with Parmesan cheese. Bake uncovered for 30 to 35 minutes or until heated through. Let stand about 10 minutes before cutting and serving.

Variation:

Omit the turkey for a vegetarian spaghetti casserole.

PASTA, CHICKEN, AND BROCCOLI BAKE

8 ounces pasta shells, elbows, or any type macaroni
1 cup chopped broccoli
½ cup chopped onion
¾ cup thin carrot pieces
2 cloves garlic, finely chopped
2 cups diced cooked chicken or turkey
½ teaspoon salt (optional)
2 (10¾-ounce) cans Healthy Request cream of mushroom soup
1 soup can water
½ cup fat-free Parmesan cheese
1 teaspoon minced dried parsley

SERVES 6

VERY LOW-FAT

Prep	:15
Cook	:45
Stand	:00
Total	1:00

Preheat the oven to 350 degrees. Lightly coat a 13 x 9 x 2-inch baking dish with vegetable oil cooking spray.

Bring a large pot of water to a boil. Add the macaroni and cook according to package directions until tender but still firm. Drain.

In a large deep nonstick skillet, sauté the broccoli, onion, and carrot for 5 minutes or until crisp-tender. Add the garlic and cook for 1 minute. Stir in the chicken and salt if using. Add the hot cooked pasta and stir to combine.

Mix the soup and water with a wire whisk until smooth. Pour over the pasta mixture. Sprinkle Parmesan cheese and parsley over all. Bake uncovered for 45 minutes, or until bubbly.

CHICKEN-MACARONI CASSEROLE

SERVES 4

This is a good recipe for chicken or turkey left over from the holidays. When doubled or tripled, it makes a good low-fat dish to take to church functions or luncheons.

9 GRAMS FAT
ENTIRE DISH

Prep   :10
Cook   :55
Stand   :00
Total   1:05

1 to 1½ cups cut-up cooked chicken or turkey white meat
1 (7-ounce) package elbow macaroni, cooked
1 cup skim milk
1 cup shredded fat-free Cheddar cheese
1 (4-ounce) can mushroom stems and pieces, undrained
1 (2-ounce) jar diced pimientos, drained
Dash of salt and pepper if desired
1 (10¾-ounce) can Healthy Request cream of mushroom soup
¾ soup can water

Preheat the oven to 350 degrees.

In an ungreased 2-quart casserole, mix the chicken, the uncooked macaroni, skim milk, shredded cheese, mushrooms, pimientos, and salt and pepper. In a small bowl, whisk the soup and water together until smooth; stir into the casserole.

Cover tightly with a lid or aluminum foil. Bake for 55 to 60 minutes or until the macaroni is tender.

PORK AND PENNE

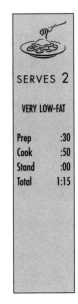

1 cup dry penne pasta
4 thinly sliced boneless center-cut pork chops
1 cup frozen green peas
2 (10¾-ounce) cans Healthy Request cream of mushroom soup
1 soup can water

SERVES 2

VERY LOW-FAT

Prep	:30
Cook	:50
Stand	:00
Total	1:15

Preheat the oven to 350 degrees. Lightly coat an 11 x 7-inch baking dish with vegetable oil cooking spray.

Bring a large saucepan of water to a boil, add the penne, and cook for 10 minutes, or until almost tender. Drain.

Trim the chops of all fat and brown on both sides in a nonstick skillet over medium heat.

Spread the pasta on the bottom of the prepared baking dish. Add the green peas as the second layer and arrange the chops on top. In a separate bowl, combine the soup and water, mix with a wire whisk, and pour over the chops. Bake uncovered until brown and bubbly, about 40 minutes.

HOT CHICKEN AND PASTA SALAD

SERVES 6

5 GRAMS FAT
ENTIRE DISH (IF
ONLY WHITE
MEAT USED)

Prep	:10
Cook	:12
Stand	:00
Total	:22

1 cup chopped broccoli
½ cup chopped onion
2 cloves garlic, finely chopped
1 cup very thin carrot strips
2 cups cut-up cooked chicken or turkey
Dash of salt (optional)
2 medium-size ripe tomatoes, chopped
8 ounces dry macaroni shells, or elbows, or choice of pasta
¼ cup fat-free Parmesan cheese
1 teaspoon snipped parsley

Heat ¼ cup of water in a medium nonstick skillet and sauté the broccoli, onion, garlic, and carrot, stirring often, for 7 to 8 minutes or just crisp-tender. Stir in the chicken and salt; heat just until hot. Add the tomatoes last so as not to overcook them. Remove from the heat, cover, and keep warm while you cook the pasta.

Bring a large pot of water to a boil. Add the macaroni and boil for 8 to 10 minutes or according to package directions, until tender but still firm. Drain and turn into a serving dish. Spoon the hot sauce over the hot pasta and sprinkle with Parmesan and parsley.

Pizza,
Polenta,
and
Bread

QUICK VEGETABLE PIZZA

1 prebaked pizza shell (see instructions page 88)
1 cup shredded fat-free Cheddar cheese
1 (16-ounce) package frozen broccoli, carrots, and red peppers, thawed
1 cup shredded fat-free mozzarella cheese
1 teaspoon crushed dried basil leaves or Italian seasoning

Preheat the oven to 400 degrees. Place the prebaked shell in a pizza pan or on a cookie sheet. Top with an even sprinkling of ½ cup of the Cheddar cheese, then all the vegetables. Sprinkle with the remaining cheeses and the seasoning. Bake for 10 to 12 minutes or until the cheese is melted.

SERVES 4

1.75 GRAMS
FAT PER SERVING
IF QUICK PIZZA
CRUST RECIPE IS
USED (PAGE
87); 3.05 IF
BASIC PIZZA
CRUST RECIPE ON
PAGE 88 IS
USED

Prep	:05
Cook	:12
Stand	:00
Total	:17

COOL SUMMER PIZZA

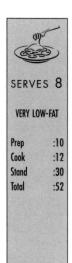

SERVES 8

VERY LOW-FAT

Prep	:10
Cook	:12
Stand	:30
Total	:52

1 prebaked pizza crust
$\frac{1}{2}$ cup fat-free sour cream
4 ounces fat-free cream cheese, softened
2 tablespoons chopped fresh parsley
1 $\frac{1}{2}$ cups chopped cooked chicken
$\frac{3}{4}$ cup chopped cooked broccoli
$\frac{3}{4}$ cup chopped seeded ripe tomato
$\frac{1}{4}$ cup chopped red onion
$\frac{1}{2}$ cup chopped yellow or green bell pepper
$\frac{1}{2}$ cup fat-free Italian dressing

Prepare a pizza crust of your choice and bake until golden brown (see prebaking instructions on page 88). Cool slightly; refrigerate about 30 minutes. (Wait until the pan is cool before placing it in the refrigerator or it will sweat and become soggy.)

Meanwhile, combine the sour cream and cream cheese; stir gently to blend until smooth. Stir in the parsley and spread the mixture over the chilled pizza crust. Top with the remaining ingredients except Italian dressing. Just before serving, drizzle dressing over the pizza. To serve, cut into pizza wedges.

CORNMEAL PIZZA

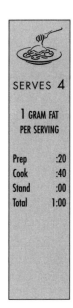

1 cup yellow cornmeal
1 1/3 cups water
1/4 cup plus 3 tablespoons Parmesan cheese (fat-free of course)
1 medium-size yellow onion, sliced thin
1 clove garlic, minced
1 small green pepper, chopped
4 medium-size mushrooms, sliced thin
3/4 teaspoon crumbled dried basil
3/4 teaspoon crumbled dried oregano
1/8 teaspoon black pepper
1 cup shredded fat-free mozzarella cheese
1 (8-ounce) can tomato sauce

SERVES 4

1 GRAM FAT
PER SERVING

Prep	:20
Cook	:40
Stand	:00
Total	1:00

Preheat the oven to 375 degrees. Lightly coat a 12-inch pizza pan or a baking sheet with olive oil cooking spray.

In a small bowl, mix the cornmeal with 2/3 cup of the cold water; in a small heavy saucepan, bring the other 2/3 cup of water to a boil. Gradually add the cornmeal mixture to the boiling water, whisking constantly with a fork until it is thick, about 5 minutes. Remove from the heat; stir in 2 tablespoons of Parmesan cheese. With wet hands, pat the cornmeal mixture evenly onto the prepared pan.

Bake the cornmeal crust uncovered for 15 to 20 minutes or until just golden brown.

In a heavy nonstick skillet, sprayed lightly with olive oil spray, sauté the onion, garlic, and green pepper for about 2 to 3 minutes. Add the mushrooms, basil, oregano, and black pepper. Cook for about 5 additional minutes.

After removing the crust from the oven, lower the heat to 350 degrees. Sprinkle half the mozzarella cheese and half the remaining Parmesan cheese over the crust. Spoon the vegetable mixture on top, pour the tomato sauce over evenly, and scatter the rest of the cheeses over the tomato sauce.

Bake for 10 to 15 minutes or until the cheese has melted. Cut into wedges.

ITSY BITSY TEENY WEENY PIZZAS

These are fun appetizers, as well as nice for small children, who really like the little pizzas they can handle all by themselves.

SERVES 4

0 GRAMS FAT
PER SERVING

Prep	:15
Cook	:10
Stand	:00
Total	:25

16 mini bagels split in half
1½ cups prepared pasta sauce
Italian seasoning
½ cup chopped onion
½ cup chopped green pepper
2 slices 99% fat-free ham, shredded very fine
1 cup shredded fat-free mozzarella cheese
1 cup shredded fat-free Parmesan cheese

Preheat the oven to 400 degrees.

Place the bagels cut side up on a baking sheet. Spread about 1 tablespoon of pasta sauce on each half. Very lightly sprinkle a pinch of Italian seasoning over each half. Place a little of the chopped onion, pepper, and ham on each. Mix the cheeses and sprinkle about a teaspoon on each pizza. Bake for about 10 minutes or until the cheese melts and the ingredients are nice and hot.

LASAGNE PIZZA PIE

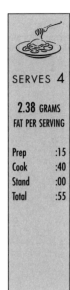

8 lasagne noodles
2 tablespoons light ricotta cheese
½ teaspoon Italian seasoning
1 (26-ounce) jar prepared pasta sauce
¾ cup broccoli florets
½ cup chopped green pepper
½ cup chopped onion
7 ounces fat-free smoked sausage, sliced thin like pepperoni
1 (8-ounce) package shredded fat-free mozzarella cheese

SERVES 4

2.38 GRAMS
FAT PER SERVING

Prep	:15
Cook	:40
Stand	:00
Total	:55

Cook the lasagne noodles in a large pot of boiling water for about 10 minutes; do not overcook. Drain; hang the noodles over the edge of a large bowl to cool (and to keep from sticking together). Meanwhile, preheat the oven to 375 degrees.

In a small bowl, mix the ricotta cheese, Italian seasoning, and 2 tablespoons of the pasta sauce. Set aside.

In a nonstick skillet with about ⅓ cup of water, sauté the broccoli, pepper, onion, and sausage just long enough to cook out the water, leaving the vegetables crisp-tender. Remove from the heat. Assemble your pizza.

Mist a pizza pan with vegetable oil cooking spray. Arrange the noodles to make a crust, overlapping just a tiny bit. Cut a noodle in half and fill in space at the end of one that is too short, and so forth. If you have noodles hanging over, take scissors and trim them off against the pan edge.

Spread a thin layer of pasta sauce over the noodles, then spread the sausage and vegetable mixture over evenly. Scatter ¾ of the mozzarella cheese over the vegetables and make a layer of pasta sauce over the cheese. Sprinkle the remaining cheese over all.

Bake uncovered for about 35 to 45 minutes, or until the desired doneness.

BISCUIT PIZZA

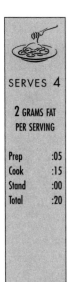

SERVES 4

2 GRAMS FAT
PER SERVING

Prep	:05
Cook	:15
Stand	:00
Total	:20

1 package refrigerated low-fat biscuits (read your labels)
½ to ¾ cup pasta sauce
⅛ teaspoon Italian seasoning
½ to ¾ cup shredded fat-free mozzarella cheese

Preheat the oven to 375 degrees.

Coat an 8-inch round baking dish with vegetable oil cooking spray. Arrange biscuits in the dish, pressing them lightly to cover the bottom and up the sides. Spread sauce, as much or little as you desire over the biscuits, sprinkle with seasoning, and top with cheese. Bake uncovered until the biscuits are golden brown and the cheese is melted and bubbly, 10 to 15 minutes.

Variation:

You may add any veggies you desire, such as onion, pepper, broccoli, your choice.

VEGETABLE PIZZA

1 recipe Basic Pizza Crust (page 88), unbaked
Prepared pasta sauce
Pizza toppings: chopped green bell pepper, chopped onion or sliced
green onions, sliced fresh or drained canned mushrooms, chopped
or sliced olives
Shredded fat-free mozzarella cheese
Grated fat-free Parmesan cheese

MAKES 2
PIZZAS

3.05 GRAMS
FAT PER SERVING

Prep	:10
Cook	:45
Stand	:00
Total	:55

Preheat the oven to 400 degrees. Spray 2 pizza pans with olive oil cooking spray and fit half the rolled-out dough in each of the pans.

Pour the desired amount of pasta sauce on the crust dough and spread evenly. Top with any or all of the toppings listed, or use your imagination and add any vegetable you like.

Bake for 30 to 45 minutes or until the vegetables are tender. Sprinkle with mozzarella and a little Parmesan and return to the oven for another 5 minutes, or until the cheese is melted.

Variation:

Add turkey sausage, cooked and drained, and rinsed with hot water, or shredded 99% fat-free ham or fat-free smoked sausage, sliced thin.

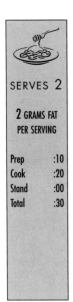

LAZY DAZE PIZZA

SERVES 2

2 GRAMS FAT
PER SERVING

Prep	:10
Cook	:20
Stand	:00
Total	:30

2 cups Stove Top instant stuffing mix, any flavor
2 tablespoons fat-free liquid-type margarine
²/₃ cup hot water
1 to 1½ cups prepared spaghetti sauce, low-fat of course
Sliced or chopped vegetables such as onion, pepper, zucchini,
    mushrooms, etc.
Fat-free mozzarella cheese, shredded (about 1 cup)

Preheat the oven to 350 degrees. Lightly spray a 9-inch round baking pan with vegetable oil cooking spray.

Combine the stuffing mix, margarine, and water. Stir until moistened. Spread the mixture evenly in the prepared pan, pressing lightly. Pour the spaghetti sauce over.

Sauté the desired vegetables in about ¼ cup of water until crisp-tender. Drain if necessary and spoon onto the pizza.

Bake for 15 minutes before topping with fat-free mozzarella cheese. Bake about 5 minutes longer to melt the cheese.

PIZZA/CALZONE DOUGH

1 package active dry yeast
1 cup lukewarm water
1 tablespoon sugar
2 tablespoons light vegetable oil
1 teaspoon salt
3 to 3¼ cups all-purpose flour

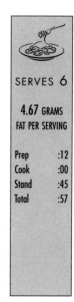

SERVES 6

4.67 GRAMS
FAT PER SERVING

Prep	:12
Cook	:00
Stand	:45
Total	:57

In a large mixing bowl, dissolve the yeast in the warm water. Stir in the sugar, oil, salt, and 1 cup of the flour. Beat until smooth. Mix in enough remaining flour, ½ cup at a time, to make the dough easy to handle.

Turn the dough out onto a floured surface and knead until smooth and elastic, about 5 minutes. Place in a glass or metal bowl lightly sprayed with vegetable oil cooking spray; turn over so the greased side is up. Cover with a kitchen towel and allow to rise until almost double in size, about 30 to 45 minutes.

For Calzone: Cut the dough into 6 equal pieces and pat out 7- or 8-inch circles.

For Pizza: Roll out to desired size on a floured surface.

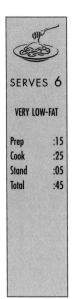

TURKEY CALZONES

SERVES 6

VERY LOW-FAT

Prep	:15
Cook	:25
Stand	:05
Total	:45

1 recipe Pizza/Calzone Dough (page 83)
³/₄ pound freshly ground lean turkey
¹/₃ cup chopped onion
1 (2-ounce) can mushroom pieces, drained
¹/₃ cup pizza sauce
³/₄ cup shredded fat-free mozzarella cheese
1 egg white

Prepare the calzone dough and pat into 6 circles. Set aside.

Preheat the oven to 375 degrees. Lightly coat a large baking sheet with vegetable oil cooking spray.

In a nonstick skillet, cook the turkey and onion until lightly browned. Place in a colander and rinse with the hottest water in your tap to remove all traces of fat. Shake excess water from the turkey; clean the skillet with paper towels or wash to remove excess fat. Return the turkey and onion to the skillet; add the mushroom pieces and pizza sauce. Cook the filling about 1 minute, while stirring.

With a knife, lightly score a line down the center of each dough circle. Spoon ¹/₆ of the filling on one side of the line and top with ¹/₆ of the cheese. Fold the other side of the dough over the filling and pinch the edges together so that the calzones are completely sealed. Brush with egg white. Punch a couple of holes in top with a toothpick. Arrange the calzones well apart on the prepared baking sheet. Bake for 20 to 25 minutes or until golden brown.

CHICKEN CALZONES

1 recipe Pizza/Calzone Dough (page 83)
1 cup cut-up cooked chicken white meat
1 1/2 cups shredded fat-free Swiss cheese
1/4 cup grated fat-free Parmesan cheese
3/4 cup chopped onion
1 clove garlic, minced
1/2 teaspoon dried thyme leaves
1 (10 3/4-ounce) can Healthy Request cream of chicken soup
1 (10-ounce) package frozen chopped spinach, thawed and
squeezed dry
1/4 cup egg substitute

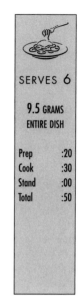

SERVES 6

9.5 GRAMS
ENTIRE DISH

Prep	:20
Cook	:30
Stand	:00
Total	:50

Prepare the calzone dough and pat into 6 circles. Set aside.

Preheat the oven to 375 degrees. Lightly coat a large baking sheet with vegetable oil cooking spray.

In a mixing bowl, combine the chicken, Swiss and Parmesan cheeses, onion, garlic, and thyme. Stir in the soup and spinach and mix until thoroughly combined.

With a knife, lightly score a line down the center of each dough circle. Spoon about 2/3 cup of the filling on one side of the line and fold the other side of the dough over the filling. Pinch the edges of the dough together so that the calzones are completely sealed. Brush with egg substitute and punch a couple of holes in the top with a toothpick. Arrange the calzones well apart on the prepared baking sheet. Bake for 25 to 30 minutes or until golden brown.

VEGETABLE CALZONES

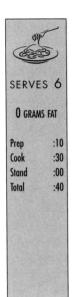

SERVES 6

0 GRAMS FAT

Prep   :10
Cook   :30
Stand   :00
Total   :40

1 recipe Pizza/Calzone dough (page 83)
1 (10-ounce) package frozen chopped broccoli
½ cup fat-free creamy Italian dressing
Dash of salt (optional)
½ (6-ounce) package fat-free cream cheese
¾ cup sliced mushrooms or 1 (4½ ounce) jar, drained
1 carrot, shredded
¼ cup chopped green pepper
1 small tomato, chopped and drained
¼ cup egg substitute

Prepare the calzone dough and pat into 6 circles. Set aside.

Preheat the oven to 375 degrees. Lightly coat a large baking sheet with vegetable oil cooking spray.

Place the broccoli in a colander under cold running water to separate the pieces; drain well.

In a mixing bowl, combine the dressing, salt (if using), and cream cheese. Stir carefully with a wire whisk just until combined —remember that fat-free cream cheese breaks down if beaten too vigorously. The sauce will appear curdled, but this is OK. Stir in the broccoli, mushrooms, carrot, green pepper, tomato, and egg substitute and mix with the sauce.

With a knife, lightly score a line down the center of each dough circle. Spoon about ⅔ cup of the vegetable mixture on one side of the line and fold the other side of the dough over the filling. Crimp the edges together so that the edges are completely sealed. Punch a few holes in the tops with a toothpick.

Arrange the calzones well apart on the prepared baking sheet. Bake for 25 to 30 minutes or until golden brown.

QUICK PIZZA CRUST

1⅔ cups all-purpose flour
1 package quick-rising dry yeast
½ cup very warm water (120 to 130 degrees—not hot or boiling)
1 teaspoon olive oil

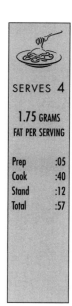

SERVES 4

1.75 GRAMS
FAT PER SERVING

Prep	:05
Cook	:40
Stand	:12
Total	:57

    Blend together ¾ cup of the flour and all the yeast in a medium-size mixing bowl. Add the water and oil; mix well. Gradually add the remaining flour and stir until a dough forms. Knead on a lightly floured surface for about 5 minutes, or until smooth and elastic. Add a little flour if the dough becomes too sticky.

    Lightly coat a clean mixing bowl with vegetable oil cooking spray. Place the dough in the bowl and turn to coat with oil. Cover the bowl with a kitchen towel and allow the dough to rest for 10 to 12 minutes before patting out into the desired shape.

Sicilian Pizza Crust:

    Mix in with the flour ¼ teaspoon each of dried thyme, crumbled dried sage, and chopped dried rosemary.

BASIC PIZZA CRUST

MAKES 2
CRUSTS

3.05 GRAMS
FAT PER SERVING

Prep   :25
Cook   :15
Stand   1:30
Total   2:10

This is a good recipe to use if you do not have a pizza pan or are serving a large group. It produces enough dough to line 2 large cookie sheets.

1 package active dry yeast
1½ cups warm (not hot) water (105 to 115 degrees)
1 teaspoon salt
2 tablespoons canola oil
4½ cups all-purpose flour, approximately

In a large mixing bowl, sprinkle the yeast over the warm water and allow to soften for 5 to 10 minutes. Add the salt and oil and 3 cups of flour; mix well. Add more flour, ½ cup at a time, beating with a wooden spoon, until you have a soft dough that is no longer sticky. Turn out onto a floured surface and knead for 8 to 10 minutes, until the dough is smooth and elastic.

Turn the dough into a clean bowl sprayed with vegetable oil cooking spray; spray the top lightly, cover with a kitchen towel, and allow to rise for 1 to 1½ hours, or until doubled in size.

Punch the dough down, divide in half, and allow to rest for 15 minutes. Roll or pat out on a floured surface as thick or thin as desired.

Prebaked Pizza Crust:

Place half the rolled-out dough on a cookie sheet or pizza pan sprayed with vegetable oil cooking spray. Bake in a 450-degree oven for 15 to 20 minutes, or until golden.

POLENTA

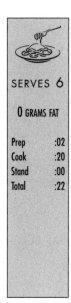

Polenta is the Italian version of cornmeal mush. It can be eaten hot with fat-free margarine and fat-free cheese. It is used in many dishes and to accompany many dishes. It can be broiled, fried, or sliced and baked with a variety of fillings.

SERVES 6

0 GRAMS FAT

6½ to 7 cups water
1 teaspoon salt
2 cups yellow cornmeal

Prep	:02
Cook	:20
Stand	:00
Total	:22

Bring the water to a boil in a large heavy pan. Add the salt and turn the heat down to low or medium low, so the water is just simmering. Start adding the cornmeal in a *very* thin stream, so thin you can see through it. Use your fist: Get a fistful of cornmeal and let it stream out between your fingers very slowly while you stir with a long strong wooden spoon. *Never* stop stirring; keep the water at a low steady simmer.

When all the cornmeal has been added, continue stirring over low heat for at least 20 minutes. When the polenta is done, it pulls away from the sides of the pot as you stir. Pour the polenta onto a large wooden chopping block or a platter. Let it cool if you are going to use it in another dish, or serve it piping hot. If some sticks to the bottom of your pan, pour a couple cups of water in and return to the burner. It will loosen in just a few minutes.

FRIED POLENTA

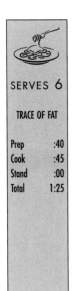

SERVES 6

TRACE OF FAT

Prep	:40
Cook	:45
Stand	:00
Total	1:25

1 recipe Polenta (page 89)
½ to ¾ cup egg substitute
1 cup Italian-style bread crumbs

Prepare the polenta as directed in the basic recipe and allow it to cool completely. (I usually make it ahead; it's better if cold.) Slice the polenta about ½ inch thick. Dip into the egg substitute, then coat with bread crumbs, shaking off the excess crumbs. Place on a baking sheet that you have sprayed with vegetable oil cooking spray. Lightly spray the tops of each piece. Bake in a 400-degree oven for about 20 minutes on each side, or until brown; turn each one over with a spatula about halfway through your cooking time.

Fried Cheese Polenta:

When ready to use, cover each one with your favorite cheese and broil until cheese is melted. Cut into individual bite-size pieces for antipasto. Serve with a piece of fresh vegetable or olives on top.

GARLIC TOAST

Thick slices of french bread, or bread of your choice
(watch for grams)
Garlic salt or garlic powder

Spray both sides of the bread with olive oil or vegetable oil cooking spray. Any type of bread will be fine; just be careful of the fat gram count per slice. Sprinkle garlic powder or garlic salt over both sides of the slices after you have sprayed them. On a large nonstick skillet or grill, brown your toast on both sides. It will look and taste just like the real fat-full thing. I won't tell if you don't; they will never know.

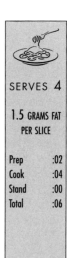

SERVES 4

1.5 GRAMS FAT
PER SLICE

Prep	:02
Cook	:04
Stand	:00
Total	:06

CHEESE AND TOMATO TOAST

4 slices Italian bread, about 1 inch thick
4 slices fat-free mozzarella cheese
2 medium-size tomatoes, sliced thin
1/8 teaspoon garlic powder
1 tablespoon fat-free Parmesan cheese

Preheat the broiler. Arrange the bread slices on a baking sheet and spray the tops with vegetable oil cooking spray. Place about 4 inches from the heat source and broil until lightly browned.

Using tongs, turn the bread over and place a cheese slice on each piece. Broil just until the cheese starts to melt. Cover the cheese with tomato slices. Mix the garlic powder and Parmesan; sprinkle lightly over the tomato slices and broil 1 minute or until heated through.

SERVES 4

1 GRAM FAT
PER SERVING

Prep	:02
Cook	:03
Stand	:00
Total	:05

Entrees

ITALIAN SEASONED LAMB CHOPS

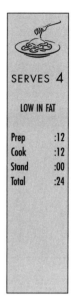

4 lean shoulder lamb chops, trimmed of all fat
1 clove garlic, crushed
¼ cup dry red wine
2 tablespoons red wine vinegar
½ teaspoon dried basil
¼ teaspoon salt
⅛ teaspoon pepper
Garlic Mint Sauce (page 175) (optional)

SERVES 4

LOW IN FAT

Prep	:12
Cook	:12
Stand	:00
Total	:24

In a large nonstick skillet, sprayed lightly with olive oil cooking spray, cook the lamb chops over medium-high heat, turning once or twice, until browned outside and partially cooked through, about 5 to 6 minutes.

Reduce the heat to medium and add the garlic, wine, vinegar, basil, salt, and pepper. Cover and simmer, turning the chops once, about 6 minutes. Remove chops to a serving platter. If desired, pass garlic mint sauce in a sauceboat.

LAMB CHOPS WITH ROSEMARY

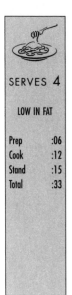

SERVES 4

LOW IN FAT

Prep	:06
Cook	:12
Stand	:15
Total	:33

8 (1-inch-thick) loin lamb chops (4 ounces each)
4 tablespoons honey mustard (fat-free)
1 clove garlic, crushed
1½ teaspoons rosemary, chopped fine or crumbled
Salt and pepper to taste

Remove any excess fat from lamb chops. In a small bowl combine the honey mustard, garlic, rosemary, salt, and pepper. Spread over both sides of the chops. Let stand at room temperature for at least 15 minutes before cooking.

Meanwhile, light a grill and preheat to medium hot. (Or preheat the oven broiler.) Grill the chops until browned outside but still pink and juicy inside, about 10 to 12 minutes for medium-rare.

If broiling inside, cook the chops 4 to 6 inches from the heat, turning once.

PORK ARROSTO (ROAST)

In Italy this is usually served on a special day or as a Sunday treat.

1 boneless pork loin roast, about 3 to 4 pounds, trimmed of all visible fat, rolled, and tied
6 garlic cloves, cut in half
3 bay leaves
¾ teaspoon salt
Dash of pepper
1 teaspoon olive oil
1 cup dry Marsala or dry sherry
½ cup water

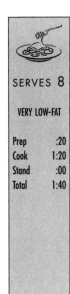

SERVES 8

VERY LOW-FAT

Prep	:20
Cook	1:20
Stand	:00
Total	1:40

Preheat the oven to 425 degrees. With a sharp knife, make 12 slits in the pork roast and stud with the garlic. Slip bay leaves under the string around the roast. Place the pork in a small roasting pan and rub the roast with salt, pepper, and olive oil

Roast the meat for 20 minutes; turn the oven down to 350 degrees and roast for about 1 additional hour, turning once or twice. Remove the meat to carving board. Cover with foil to keep warm.

Pour off any fat in the pan. Place the pan over a burner on low heat. Add the Marsala or sherry and water; bring to a boil, scraping up the browned bits from the bottom of the pan. Boil until the liquid is reduced to ¾ cup, about 5 minutes.

Remove the string and bay leaves from the roast. Slice the pork and drizzle the pan juices over the meat.

HAM-STUFFED ZUCCHINI

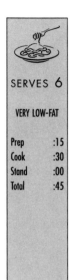

SERVES 6

VERY LOW-FAT

Prep	:15
Cook	:30
Stand	:00
Total	:45

3 medium zucchini
¼ cup chopped onion
½ cup finely chopped prosciutto or 99 percent fat-free ham
¼ cup soft bread crumbs
½ teaspoon dried parsley
½ cup grated fat-free Parmesan cheese
¼ cup egg substitute
¼ teaspoon salt
⅛ teaspoon grated nutmeg

Preheat the oven to 350 degrees. Lightly spray a baking dish with olive oil cooking spray.

Trim the ends from the zucchini but leave them whole. Cook them in a large saucepan of boiling salted water for 2 to 3 minutes; drain and rinse under cold running water. Cut the zucchini in half lengthwise. Scoop out the center of each zucchini, making a boat with sides about ¼ inch thick. Chop the zucchini centers that you have removed.

In a large nonstick skillet, sauté onion in about ⅛ cup water just until crisp-tender. Stir in the prosciutto, chopped zucchini, bread crumbs, and parsley. Cook, stirring often, for about 2 more minutes. Remove from the heat and stir in ¼ cup of the Parmesan cheese, egg substitute, salt, and nutmeg.

Fill the zucchini boats with the bread crumb mixture. Place in the prepared baking dish and lightly spray the top with olive oil cooking spray. Sprinkle the remaining ¼ cup of Parmesan cheese over the boats. Bake for 20 minutes or until heated through. You may want to broil for 1 or 2 minutes to brown the tops.

ITALIAN SAUSAGE BAKE

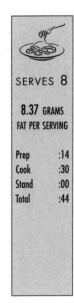

1 pound Italian-style bulk turkey sausage (or link sausage removed from skins)
¾ cup chopped onion
2 (10¾-ounce) cans fat-free condensed cream of mushroom soup, such as Healthy Request
2½ cups skim milk
1 teaspoon Italian seasoning
2 cups frozen hash brown potatoes, with peppers and onions or plain
2 cups reduced-fat Bisquick
2 tablespoons dried parsley (optional)

SERVES 8

8.37 GRAMS
FAT PER SERVING

Prep	:14
Cook	:30
Stand	:00
Total	:44

Preheat the oven to 400 degrees. Lightly coat a 13 x 9 x 2-inch baking pan with vegetable oil cooking spray.

Brown the sausage and onions together in a nonstick skillet, stirring to break up lumps. Place in a colander and rinse off the fat with the hottest water available. Shake excess water off. Set aside.

In a mixing bowl, combine the soup with 1 cup of the milk, the Italian seasoning, and the potatoes. Stir in the sausage. Mix well. Pour into the prepared baking dish.

In a separate mixing bowl, combine the biscuit mix with the remaining 1½ cups of milk. Spread over the meat and potato mixture. Sprinkle with parsley if desired. Bake uncovered for 25 to 30 minutes or until the crust is lightly browned.

Variation:

Substitute 2¼ cups mixed vegetables for the potatoes.

SAUSAGE AND BEAN BAKE

SERVES 4

1 GRAM FAT
PER SERVING

Prep	:10
Cook	:45
Stand	:00
Total	:55

8 ounces fat-free smoked turkey sausage
1½ cups chopped onion
2 cloves garlic, chopped fine
2 boneless skinless chicken breast halves, cut into 1-inch pieces
2 (14½ ounce) cans diced tomatoes
1 (15-ounce) can Great Northern beans, drained and rinsed
1 (15-ounce) can red kidney beans, drained and rinsed
1 cup fat-free chicken broth
1½ cups thinly sliced carrots
¾ cup finely chopped celery
1 teaspoon dried thyme
1 tablespoon fresh snipped parsley or 1 teaspoon dried

Preheat the oven to 375 degrees. Lightly spray a 13 x 9 x 2-inch casserole with vegetable oil cooking spray.

Over medium heat, in a nonstick skillet or saucepan, cook the sausage, onion, and garlic, stirring often, for about 3 minutes. Add the chicken, and stir until browned and cooked through, about 12 to 14 minutes. Stir in the tomatoes, beans, broth, carrots, celery, and thyme.

Spoon the mixture into the prepared casserole and cover with a lid or aluminum foil. Bake for about 25 to 30 minutes. Stir in the parsley.

Note: If serving only two people, divide the mixture between two one-quart casseroles. Wrap one with foil; label and freeze for up to three weeks.

SAUSAGE-EGGPLANT LASAGNE

2 small eggplants
1 (16-ounce) package fat-free turkey bulk breakfast turkey sausage
½ chopped green pepper
½ cup chopped onion
¾ cup finely chopped yellow summer squash
1½ cups low-fat pasta sauce, such as Healthy Choice
4 to 6 tablespoons fat-free ricotta cheese
½ cup shredded fat-free mozzarella cheese
1 tablespoon pizza seasoning
½ teaspoon minced garlic
½ cup grated fat-free Parmesan cheese

SERVES 6

9.0 GRAMS FAT
PER SERVINGS

Prep	:12
Cook	:55
Stand	:15
Total	1:22

Preheat the oven to 350 degrees. Lightly spray an 11 x 7-inch baking dish with vegetable oil cooking spray.

Cut the eggplants lengthwise into ½-inch-thick slices; place in a large bowl and cover with salt water (about 2 tablespoons of salt to 2 or 3 quarts of water). This will help prevent discoloring of the eggplant.

Brown the sausages in a nonstick skillet along with the peppers and onions. Add the squash when about halfway done. Using a plastic spatula or a wooden spoon, cut the sausages into small pieces. When done, place in a colander and rinse with your hottest water from the tap. (This will help to wash away more fat grams that cooked out of the sausage.) Shake the sausage to remove any excess water.

Spread 4 to 6 tablespoons of the pasta sauce over the bottom of the prepared baking dish. Drain the eggplant slices and blot them dry. Place 4 over the bottom, or enough to cover the bottom of the baking dish. Layer the sausage over the eggplant. Spoon over the eggplant about ¼ cup of pasta sauce; next, add the ricotta cheese and ½ cup of mozzarella. Place another layer of eggplant, the pizza seasoning, minced garlic, and remaining pasta sauce over all. Sprinkle with the Parmesan cheese.

Bake uncovered for about 45 minutes or until the casserole is bubbly and done to knife test. Allow to stand about 15 minutes before cutting.

BLACK-EYED PEAS AND SAUSAGE
WITH TOMATO SAUCE

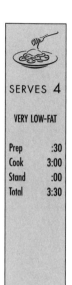

SERVES 4

VERY LOW-FAT

Prep	:30
Cook	3:00
Stand	:00
Total	3:30

1 teaspoon olive oil
¼ cup chopped yellow onion
¼ teaspoon chopped garlic
⅓ cup chopped carrots
⅓ cup chopped celery
1 cup canned Italian tomatoes, coarsely chopped, with juice
1 pound any light or low-fat sweet or breakfast sausage
1 cup dried black-eyed peas, soaked in warm water 1 hour
Salt and pepper to taste

In a kettle or heavy ovenproof saucepan, heat the olive oil, add the onion, and sauté over medium heat until pale gold. Add the garlic and sauté until lightly colored. Add the carrots and celery; cook for 4 or 5 minutes. Turn the heat down to low, add the chopped tomatoes with their juice, and cook at a gentle low simmer for about 20 minutes.

Preheat the oven to 350 degrees.

In a nonstick skillet, brown the sausage, crumbling with a spoon as it cooks. Place in a colander and run the hottest water from your tap over it, shaking to move the sausage around and rinse away all possible fat. (If using sausage links, puncture them in several places and add to the kettle; continue to cook for about 15 more minutes. If using a smoked type of sausage, cut into pieces about 2 inches in length and add to the kettle; continue to cook for about 15 minutes.) After rinsing the crumbled sausage, shake until well drained and add to the kettle of cooking vegetables; continue to cook for about 5 minutes.

Drain the peas; add to the kettle along with enough water to cover them well. Bring to a steady simmer. Transfer to the middle level of the preheated oven and cook uncovered for 1½ to 2 hours, or until the peas are tender. Cooking time will vary according to the peas. Be sure to check occasionally to see if additional water is needed. When done, if the mixture is watery, return to the stovetop and bring to a boil; simmer until the liquid is concentrated. Season with salt and pepper to taste.

Spoon off the fat, or better yet, refrigerate overnight, lift off the fat that comes to the top, reheat, and serve.

Variation:

Substitute a 15-ounce can of cannellini beans, drained and rinsed. Shorten the oven-cooking time to 45 minutes or until the vegetables are tender.

Note: This can be cooked on stovetop; just continue to simmer until done to desired consistency. It makes a good do-ahead dish and you can lift off more fat by refrigerating overnight.

SPICY SAUSAGE AND CABBAGE CASSEROLE

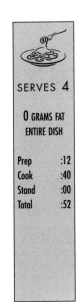

¼ cup chopped onion
⅛ teaspoon chopped garlic
1 small green pepper, chopped
1 (14-ounce) package fat-free smoked sausage (such as Butterball)
2½ cups chopped cabbage
1 (14½-ounce) can diced Italian-style tomatoes

SERVES 4

0 GRAMS FAT
ENTIRE DISH

Prep	:12
Cook	:40
Stand	:00
Total	:52

Preheat the oven to 350 degrees. Lightly spray an 11 x 7-inch baking dish with vegetable oil cooking spray.

In a medium-size nonstick skillet, sauté the onion, garlic, and pepper in about ¼ cup of water; when about half tender, add the sausage, sliced lengthwise and then cut into 1-inch pieces. (It really doesn't matter how you want to cut it up.) Sauté for about 2 minutes; add the cabbage and about ¼ cup more water. Sauté while stirring until the cabbage is crisp-tender. Don't cook too long —cabbage needs to keep some texture.

Pour the cabbage and sausage into the prepared baking dish. Pour the tomatoes, juice and all, evenly over the mixture. Bake uncovered for about 35 minutes.

Note: This can be made a day ahead. Cover with foil and refrigerate until time to bake.

SMOKED SAUSAGE, VEGETABLES, AND PASTA ITALIANO

SERVES 4

1 GRAM FAT
PER SERVING

Prep	:15
Cook	:35
Stand	:00
Total	:50

1½ cups, dry small tube pasta, such as elbows
7 ounces fat-free smoked link sausage, such as Butterball
⅔ cup chopped onion
⅔ cup chopped green pepper
1½ cups frozen green peas
1 cup chopped yellow summer squash
1 (14-ounce) can diced tomatoes with roasted garlic, onion, and oregano
1½ teaspoons Italian seasoning
Ground black pepper to taste

In a medium saucepan, cook the pasta according to package directions, leaving out any oil or salt called for. Drain and set aside.

Cut the sausage in half lengthwise, then slice thin into little half moons.

In a large nonstick skillet, sauté the onion, pepper, and sausage until the sausage is lightly browned. Add the peas, squash, and undrained tomatoes. Sprinkle on the Italian seasoning and desired amount of pepper. Stir to blend well. Mix in the pasta and simmer for about 5 minutes over low heat, stirring occasionally.

Oregano

Oregano did not become a staple in American kitchens until after World War II. Also known as wild marjoram, it was first grown and used primarily for medicinal purposes.

Oregano is difficult to raise. A perennial that in ideal circumstances will grow to about two feet high, it needs to be in a sunny spot with well-drained soil.

Oregano is ideal in all kinds of tomato dishes, especially such Italian recipes as spaghetti sauce, pizza, and lasagne. Its peppery flavor enhances egg and cheese dishes. Soups as well as many other dishes also benefit from the addition of oregano.

SAUSAGE AND RIGATONI BAKE

This crowd pleaser is a great dish for family night at church.

1½ pounds dried rigatoni
1½ cups chopped onion
2 pounds bulk turkey sausage
2 (30-ounce) cans Italian crushed tomatoes in purée
2 teaspoons dried basil
1 teaspoon dried oregano
1 teaspoon dried parsley
1 pound fat-free mozzarella cheese, shredded
1½ cups grated fat-free Parmesan cheese

SERVES
10

6 GRAMS FAT
PER SERVING

Prep	:15
Cook	1:25
Stand	:00
Total	1:40

Bring a large kettle of salted water to boil, add the rigatoni, and cook 10 to 12 minutes or according to package directions. Drain, rinse under cool water, and drain again.

In a nonstick saucepan or large skillet, sauté the onion in ¼ cup of water for 2 to 3 minutes or until tender. Add the sausage, crumbling as you add; cook, stirring to break up lumps, until lightly browned. Transfer to a colander; rinse with the hottest water in your tap to remove any fat. Shake the excess water off. Meanwhile, wash the skillet or saucepan to remove any remaining fat.

Return the sausage and onion mixture to the pan, along with the tomatoes, basil, oregano, parsley, and 2 cups of water. Bring to a boil. Reduce the heat to medium; cover and cook, stirring occasionally, until the sauce thickens, 8 to 9 minutes.

Meanwhile, preheat the oven to 350 degrees. Lightly spray a 13 x 9 x 2-inch baking dish or two 9-inch square baking dishes with vegetable oil cooking spray.

In a large bowl, combine the pasta with two thirds of the sauce. Stir in the mozzarella cheese and 1 cup of the Parmesan. Pour the pasta mixture into the prepared baking dish. Cover with the remaining sauce and sprinkle with the remaining ½ cup of Parmesan. Cover with foil and bake for 25 minutes. Uncover and bake about 10 minutes longer, or until bubbly and lightly browned.

Note: You can halve this recipe and use a smaller pan. Or make the full recipe, divide into two casseroles, and freeze one for later. Remember when you are baking a frozen dish that it takes about 30 minutes longer.

GRILLED SAUSAGE KABOBS

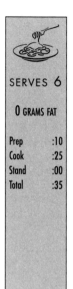

SERVES 6

0 GRAMS FAT

Prep :10
Cook :25
Stand :00
Total :35

1 teaspoon crushed dried basil
1/2 cup prepared light or fat-free pizza sauce
1 1/2 pounds fat-free smoked sausage links, cut into 1 1/2-inch pieces
2 medium zucchini, cut into 1-inch pieces
1 medium red bell pepper, cut into 1 1/2-inch squares
1 medium green bell pepper, cut into 1 1/2-inch squares

Prepare a charcoal fire or preheat a gas grill.

Mix the basil with the pizza sauce; set aside. Cook the sausage pieces over medium heat until lightly browned, about 5 minutes. Cool. Alternate pieces of sausage, pepper, and zucchini on skewers until the skewers are filled.

Place the kabobs 5 or 6 inches from the heat source, turning and brushing with the pizza sauce 2 or 3 times until the sausage is done and the vegetables are crisp-tender, 20 to 25 minutes. Placing a piece of foil over the kabobs helps to distribute the heat more evenly.

CHICKEN CACCIATORE

4 boneless skinless chicken breast halves, cut into bite-size pieces
1 cup chopped onion
3 cloves garlic, minced
1 cup dry red wine
1 (14-ounce) can Italian tomatoes, drained and chopped
1 teaspoon dried oregano
Pinch of salt
Dash of pepper
1 teaspoon dried parsley

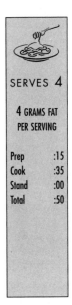

SERVES 4

4 GRAMS FAT
PER SERVING

Prep	:15
Cook	:35
Stand	:00
Total	:50

In a nonstick skillet or saucepan sprayed lightly with olive oil cooking spray, brown the chicken for 4 to 5 minutes, turning to cook all sides. Add the onion; cook about 2 more minutes or until softened. Add the garlic and cook just a half minute or so. Stir in the wine, tomatoes, and oregano. Bring to a boil, reduce the heat to medium-low, cover, and simmer for about 30 minutes. Season with salt and pepper if desired. Sprinkle with parsley just before serving. Serve over pasta.

QUICK CHICKEN CACCIATORE

SERVES 4

3 GRAMS FAT
PER SERVING

Prep	:12
Cook	:25
Stand	:00
Total	:37

4 boneless skinless chicken breast halves
1 small green bell pepper, chopped fine
1 teaspoon minced garlic
1 (26-ounce) jar low-fat spaghetti sauce, such as Healthy Choice

In a nonstick skillet, brown the chicken on both sides and continue cooking over medium heat for about 15 minutes or until tender. Using the edge of a spatula, cut the chicken into bite-size pieces. Add the green pepper and garlic and cook, stirring, for a few minutes longer. You may need to add about ¼ cup water to cook the vegetables until crisp-tender.

Add the pasta sauce and simmer until hot and bubbly. Serve over hot cooked pasta, topped with your favorite FAT-FREE cheese, such as Parmesan or provolone.

EASY CHICKEN CACCIATORE

SERVES 4

4 GRAMS FAT
PER SERVING

Prep	:15
Cook	:50
Stand	:00
Total	1:05

4 boneless skinless chicken breast halves
1 (26-ounce) jar low-fat spaghetti sauce, such as Healthy Choice
12 ounces dry spaghetti

In a nonstick skillet, brown the chicken over medium heat. There is no need to add any cooking oil or spray; the chicken will cook in its own juices. Just watch not to let it get too dry—you may need to add about ¼ cup of water to keep this from happening. When the chicken is no longer pink in the center—about 10 to 12 minutes—cut it into bite-size pieces.

Return the chicken to the skillet, pour the spaghetti sauce over, and heat slowly, stirring occasionally. If you have your heat too high, the sauce will splatter all over your stove.

Meanwhile, bring a large pot of water to a boil, add the spaghetti, and cook for 10 to 12 minutes or according to package directions. Drain and transfer to a serving bowl. Mix in the sauce and serve with a nice green salad and Garlic Toast (see recipe on page 91).

SEASONED CHICKEN

The look and appearance of fried without all the fat.

1 cup skim milk or low-fat buttermilk (1 gram fat per cup) or ½ cup egg substitute
1 cup Seasoned Crumb Mix (recipe below)
1 pound chicken tenders

SERVES **4**

CHICKEN
TENDERS
.05 GRAMS OF
FAT EACH

Prep	:05
Cook	:40
Stand	:00
Total	:45

Preheat the oven to 350 degrees.

Pour the milk into a shallow bowl. Place the crumb mixture in another bowl next to it.

Dip the chicken pieces one at a time in the milk, then in the crumbs, turning to coat evenly. As the pieces are coated, lightly spray the undersides with vegetable oil cooking spray before placing them on a nonstick baking pan. Spray the tops lightly, place in the oven, and bake for 25 to 30 minutes or until golden brown and cooked through. Turn the pieces halfway through cooking if you want them crisp and brown on both sides.

SEASONED CRUMB MIX

2½ cups cornflake crumbs
1 tablespoon parsley flakes
½ teaspoon crumbled dried rosemary or sage
½ teaspoon crumbled dried thyme or marjoram
½ teaspoon grated lemon rind

SERVES **4**

0 GRAMS FAT

Prep	:03
Cook	:00
Stand	:00
Total	:03

Place all the ingredients in a zipper-lock plastic bag or jar; shake well to mix. Use as a crumb coating for chicken or pork fillets. The mix will keep for about 2 months in the refrigerator. Makes about 2½ cups.

SKILLET PARMESAN CHICKEN BREASTS

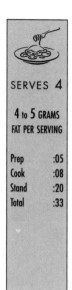

SERVES **4**

4 to **5** GRAMS
FAT PER SERVING

Prep   :05
Cook   :08
Stand   :20
Total   :33

⅓ cup fine dry bread crumbs
1 tablespoon minced fresh parsley or 1 teaspoon dried
3 tablespoons grated fat-free Parmesan cheese
2 large egg whites mixed with 2 teaspoons water
4 boneless skinless chicken breast halves, pounded to ¼ inch
   thickness
1 lemon, quartered lengthwise

Combine the bread crumbs and parsley in a pie plate or shallow bowl. Place the cheese on another plate. In a third bowl or pie plate, lightly beat the egg whites with the water.

Dip the chicken in the cheese, then into the egg whites, then into the crumb mixture, coating both sides evenly. Lay on a wire rack and refrigerate for about 20 minutes.

Heat a heavy nonstick skillet sprayed lightly with olive oil cooking spray. Add the chicken, spray the top with olive oil spray, and brown lightly on both sides. Lower the heat and cook until tender and no longer pink in the center. Transfer the chicken to a warm platter and garnish with lemon quarters. Serve a lemon wedge with each piece and squeeze a little juice on before eating.

CHICKEN ITALIAN STYLE

4 boneless skinless chicken breast halves, pounded flat
1 medium-size yellow onion, chopped
1 medium-size carrot, chopped
1 medium-size stalk celery, chopped
3 cloves garlic, minced
1 cup dry white wine
1 medium-size ripe tomato, peeled, cored, and chopped
1 bay leaf, crumbled
½ teaspoon crumbled dried basil
½ teaspoon crumbled dried thyme
¼ teaspoon ground black pepper
2 tablespoons minced fresh parsley or 1 tablespoon dried
1½ teaspoons grated lemon rind

SERVES **4**

2–3 GRAMS
FAT PER SERVING
—DEPENDING
ON CUT OF
CHICKEN

Prep	:25
Cook	1:15
Stand	:00
Total	1:40

Heat a deep nonstick skillet or 4-quart nonstick dutch oven and spray lightly with olive oil cooking spray. Brown the chicken over high heat for about 2 minutes on each side. Transfer to a platter and set aside.

Reduce the heat to medium. Put ¼ cup water in the pan and add the onion, carrot, celery, and half the garlic. Cook uncovered for 5 minutes or until the onion is soft. Add the wine and boil uncovered, stirring occasionally to loosen any browned bits, for about 5 minutes or until the liquid has boiled down by half.

Return the chicken and juices to the skillet, add tomato, bay leaf, basil, thyme, and pepper. Cover and simmer over medium to low heat for 1 to 1¼ hours or until the meat is tender but not falling to pieces.

Meanwhile, combine the parsley, lemon rind, and remaining garlic. Add to the skillet just before serving. Serve with noodles or steamed rice.

Variation:

This is also excellent with veal or pork.

ITALIAN CHICKEN

SERVES 4

3 GRAMS FAT
PER SERVING

Prep	:05
Cook	1:00
Stand	:00
Total	1:05

1 ½ cups cornflake crumbs
1 cup tomato sauce
½ teaspoon garlic salt
½ teaspoon crushed dried basil leaves
¼ teaspoon crushed dried oregano
4 boneless skinless chicken breast halves

Preheat the oven to 350 degrees. Lightly spray a shallow baking dish with vegetable oil cooking spray.

Place the cornflake crumbs in a pie plate or shallow bowl. In another pie plate or bowl, mix the tomato sauce, garlic salt, basil, and oregano.

Dip the chicken pieces in the tomato sauce mixture, then roll in the crumbs to coat. Place in the prepared baking dish and spray the top of the chicken lightly with cooking spray. Bake uncovered and without turning for 1 hour or until the chicken is tender and lightly browned.

DOUBLE DIP CHICKEN

½ cup egg substitute
½ cup skim milk
½ cup all-purpose flour
½ teaspoon seasoned salt
¼ teaspoon ground black pepper
2 cups cornflake crumbs
4 to 6 boneless skinless chicken breast halves
¼ cup fat-free liquid-form margarine such as Fleischmann's

SERVES 4

3 GRAMS FAT
PER SERVING

Prep	:05
Cook	1:15
Stand	:00
Total	1:20

Preheat the oven to 350 degrees. Spray a baking dish lightly with vegetable oil cooking spray.

Make a batter: In a shallow bowl, combine the egg substitute and milk; mix slightly. Add the flour, salt, and pepper. Mix with a wire whisk until smooth.

Place the cornflake crumbs in another shallow bowl.

Dip the chicken pieces one at a time in the batter, then roll in the crumbs until coated. Arrange on the prepared baking dish and drizzle with the margarine.

Bake uncovered for about 50 minutes or until the chicken is tender. Turn once during baking if you want both sides to be crisp.

CORNMEAL-CRUSTED CHICKEN

You might like to serve a nice fruit salsa alongside this chicken.

SERVES 4

**3 GRAMS FAT
PER SERVING**

Prep	:08
Cook	:40
Stand	:00
Total	:48

³/₄ cup cornmeal
½ teaspoon salt
Dash of pepper
½ cup egg substitute
4 boneless skinless chicken breast halves

Preheat the oven to 400 degrees. Coat an ovenproof dish with vegetable oil cooking spray.

Mix the cornmeal, salt, and pepper in a shallow dish such as a pie plate. Put the egg substitute in a similar dish.

Dip each chicken breast in the egg substitute, then roll in the cornmeal until coated. Place the chicken pieces on the prepared baking dish and spray the tops lightly. Bake for 30 to 40 minutes or until tender and crispy.

Rosemary

~ Rosemary is a native of the coasts of Spain, Portugal, France, and Italy. A hardy and drought-resistant perennial, rosemary likes sandy soil and lots of sun.
Rosemary is nice with most meats, but be careful—too much can be overpowering. Soups, potatoes, eggplant, and the like also benefit from a touch of rosemary.

GRILLED CHICKEN

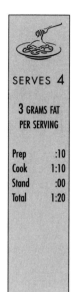

4 to 6 chicken breast halves
¼ cup fat-free Italian dressing
3 cloves garlic
2 tablespoons lemon juice
1 teaspoon Dijon mustard
1 teaspoon dried rosemary
½ teaspoon ground black pepper

SERVES 4

**3 GRAMS FAT
PER SERVING**

Prep	:10
Cook	1:10
Stand	:00
Total	1:20

Remove the skin from the chicken breasts, leaving the bone in. (It makes the chicken stay moist while grilling to have the bone in.)

In a blender container, combine the dressing, garlic, lemon juice, mustard, rosemary, and pepper; blend until smooth. Brush the chicken with the mixture; cover and refrigerate 6 to 8 hours.

Prepare a fire in a charcoal grill and bring the coals to medium heat; or preheat a gas-fired grill to medium. Place the chicken meaty side up on an oiled grill rack. Cook for 12 to 15 minutes; turn and cook for 20 to 25 minutes longer or until done.

Note: The chicken can also be baked in the oven. Preheat the oven to 400 degrees. Remove the chicken from the marinade, place the pieces on a nonstick baking pan sprayed lightly with vegetable oil cooking spray, and spray the tops. Bake uncovered for 25 to 30 minutes, until tender.

CHICKEN CUTLETS PARMIGIANA

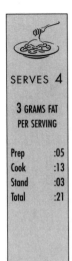

SERVES 4

3 GRAMS FAT
PER SERVING

Prep	:05
Cook	:13
Stand	:03
Total	:21

4 boneless skinless chicken breast halves
Salt and pepper to taste
1 (16-ounce) jar low-fat spaghetti sauce, such as Healthy Choice
3 tablespoons fat-free Parmesan cheese

Pound the chicken breasts to ½ inch thickness with the flat side of a meat mallet or chef's knife. Sprinkle salt and pepper over the chicken. Spray a nonstick skillet lightly with olive oil cooking spray. Heat over medium heat, add the chicken, and cook, turning to brown on both sides, about 7 to 8 minutes.

Spoon the spaghetti sauce over the chicken; continue to cook over medium heat about 5 minutes longer or until the chicken is fork tender and the sauce is bubbly. Sprinkle cheese over, cover, and let stand for 2 or 3 minutes or until the cheese melts.

Serve with hot cooked spaghetti.

CHICKEN SCALOPPINE MARSALA

4 boneless skinless chicken breast halves
½ cup egg substitute
¾ cup cornflake crumbs or cracker meal
1 tablespoon olive oil
1 clove garlic, minced
1 packet low-sodium chicken bouillon
¼ cup Marsala wine
Dash of pepper
1 tablespoon chopped fresh parsley or 1 teaspoon dried
Twist of lemon for garnish

SERVES 4

7 GRAMS FAT
PER SERVING

Prep	:15
Cook	:10
Stand	:00
Total	:25

Place the chicken pieces one at a time in an open zipper-lock plastic bag and pound to ¼ inch thickness with the flat side of a chef's knife or meat mallet. (The bag keeps things from spattering all over your kitchen.)

Put the egg substitute in a shallow bowl. Put the crumbs in a separate shallow bowl. Set aside.

Spray a large nonstick skillet with vegetable oil cooking spray. Add the olive oil and cook the garlic for 1 minute or until golden, taking care that it doesn't burn. Remove the garlic with a spoon and reserve. Dip a chicken piece in the egg substitute and then in the crumbs to coat both sides. Place in the skillet and cook over medium heat for 6 to 7 minutes, turning once, until cooked through. Remove to a serving platter and cover with foil to keep warm. Repeat with the remaining chicken pieces.

Dissolve the bouillon in ¼ cup of water and pour into the skillet along with the Marsala, pepper, parsley, and reserved garlic. Cook, stirring to get up the browned bits in the bottom of the pan, until the mixture thickens and begins to boil. Spoon the sauce over the scaloppine and serve garnished with a lemon twist.

CHICKEN-APPLE ROLLS

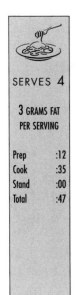

SERVES 4

3 GRAMS FAT
PER SERVING

Prep	:12
Cook	:35
Stand	:00
Total	:47

4 boneless skinless chicken breast halves
3/4 cup finely chopped apple
2 tablespoons shredded fat-free mozzarella cheese
1 tablespoon fine dry bread crumbs
1/4 cup dry white wine
1 1/2 tablespoons cornstarch
Chopped parsley for garnish

Pound the chicken to 1/4 inch thickness. (Place the pieces one at a time between two sheets of waxed paper or inside an open zipper-lock plastic bag and use the flat side of a meat mallet or chef's knife to flatten them.)

Lay the chicken pieces out on a work surface. Combine the apple, cheese, and bread crumbs. Place a portion of each down the center of each chicken breast. Roll up and secure with wooden toothpicks.

Brown the rolls in a nonstick skillet, turning to brown both sides. Spray a little vegetable oil cooking spray if you feel it is necessary, but they will brown fine without. Add the wine and 1/4 cup water; cover and simmer 15 to 20 minutes or until the chicken is tender and no longer pink.

Remove the rolls from the pan. Combine the cornstarch with 1 tablespoon of cold water; stir into the juices in the pan. Cook and stir until thickened. Pour over the rolls and garnish with parsley. Remove the toothpicks before serving.

CHICKEN CUTLETS

4 boneless skinless chicken breast halves
1 cup all-purpose flour
½ cup egg substitute mixed with 1 tablespoon water
1¼ cups Italian-flavored fine dry bread crumbs (such as Progresso)

SERVES 4

5.88 GRAMS
FAT PER CUTLET

Preheat the oven to 425 degrees. Spray a heavy baking sheet with vegetable oil cooking spray.

Place the chicken breasts, one at a time, between sheets of waxed paper or in an open plastic bag and pound to ¼ inch thickness with the flat side of a meat mallet or chef's knife. Set aside.

Put three shallow bowls or pie plates next to each other on a work surface. In one place the flour; in another the egg substitute; in another the bread crumbs.

Dredge one cutlet at a time, coating first with the flour, then dipping in the egg wash, then coating with bread crumbs. You may need to turn them a couple of times to coat well with the crumbs.

Place the cutlets on the prepared baking sheet and spray the tops with cooking spray. Bake for 20 minutes. Turn with tongs and bake 20 minutes more or until golden brown.

Prep	:20
Cook	:40
Stand	:00
Total	1:00

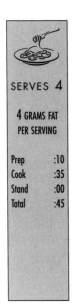

BAKED PARMESAN CHICKEN BREASTS

SERVES 4

4 GRAMS FAT
PER SERVING

Prep	:10
Cook	:35
Stand	:00
Total	:45

½ cup grated fat-free Parmesan cheese
½ cup fine dry bread crumbs
1 teaspoon crushed dried oregano
1 teaspoon crushed dried parsley
¼ teaspoon paprika
Salt and pepper to taste
½ cup egg substitute
4 boneless skinless chicken breast halves

Spray a baking sheet lightly with vegetable oil cooking spray; set aside. Heat the oven to 400 degrees.

In a pie plate or shallow bowl, combine the Parmesan with the bread crumbs, oregano, parsley, paprika, salt, and pepper. Put the egg substitute in another shallow dish.

One piece at a time, dip the chicken in the egg substitute, then roll in the crumb mixture. Place the chicken pieces on the prepared baking sheet and spray the tops with cooking spray. Bake uncovered for 25 to 30 minutes or until tender. I turn mine when about half done; this makes both sides nice and crispy brown.

CHICKEN FLORENTINE

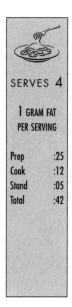

8 chicken tenders (about ¾ pound of boneless skinless white meat)
¾ cup chopped onion
1 clove garlic, minced
1 (10-ounce) package frozen chopped spinach, thawed
1 cup fat-free chicken broth
½ cup water
1 cup instant rice
⅓ cup grated fat-free Parmesan cheese

SERVES 4

1 GRAM FAT
PER SERVING

Prep	:25
Cook	:12
Stand	:05
Total	:42

Sauté the chicken in a nonstick skillet, sprayed with butter-flavored cooking oil spray, until lightly browned. When you turn the chicken over, add the onion; continue cooking until lightly browned on this side. Add the garlic and cook about 30 seconds, stirring continuously; don't burn it. (I have warned you many times about burning garlic. It only takes one time—an unforgettable experience.)

Add the spinach, broth, and water. Bring to a boil. Reduce the heat and simmer for 4 minutes, covered. Stir in the rice and cheese. Replace the cover, remove from the heat, and let stand for 5 minutes.

CHICKEN-EGGPLANT PIE

SERVES 4

2 GRAMS FAT PER SERVING

Prep	:15
Cook	:40
Stand	:00
Total	:55

Don't tell me we can't have our gravy and eat it too! This will make you think you're having Grandma's fried chicken and gravy.

1 medium eggplant, sliced into 12 rounds
1 tablespoon grated fat-free Parmesan cheese
½ teaspoon garlic powder, or 1 clove minced fresh garlic
3 boneless skinless chicken breast halves, diced
1 (14½-ounce) can diced tomatoes
1½ cups chopped onion
1 cup chopped green pepper
1 cup sliced mushrooms
¾ teaspoon Italian seasoning
Dash of ground black pepper

Place the sliced eggplant in enough salt water to cover—about 2 quarts of water to 2 tablespoons of salt. Let stand about 10 minutes while you preheat the oven to 375 degrees.

Drain the eggplant and pat dry. Arrange in one layer on a non-stick baking sheet and spray lightly with vegetable oil cooking spray. Broil about 2 minutes or until golden. Turn the slices over, spray lightly with cooking oil spray, and sprinkle with Parmesan and garlic powder mixed. Broil until golden, about 2 more minutes. Set aside.

Spray an 8-inch square baking dish lightly with vegetable oil cooking spray.

In a nonstick skillet over medium high heat, cook the chicken, stirring, until browned and cooked through. Add the tomatoes and their juice, the onion, green pepper, mushrooms, Italian seasoning, and black pepper. Stir to mix well. Bring to a boil, reduce the heat to low, and simmer for 5 minutes.

Arrange 6 eggplant slices in the bottom of the prepared baking dish to form the bottom of the pie; Top with the chicken mixture; arrange the remaining 6 eggplant slices over the chicken. Cover with foil; bake for about 30 minutes.

Note: This can be made ahead and refrigerated covered until time to bake, or it can be frozen, then baked for about 50 minutes or until heated through.

STIR-FRIED ITALIAN CHICKEN AND VEGETABLES

You can be creative and add any vegetables you desire. This is fast and nice with the Italian flavor.

SERVES 4

4 GRAMS FAT
ENTIRE DISH

Prep	:20
Cook	:12
Stand	:00
Total	:32

8 chicken tenders
1 clove garlic, minced
1 medium onion, halved lengthwise, then sliced thin crosswise
1 small green pepper, halved and cut into thin strips
1 small red bell pepper, halved and cut into thin strips
1 small eggplant, peeled and chopped into bite-size pieces
1 medium zucchini, cut into bite-size pieces
2 cups frozen broccoli cuts, thawed
½ cup frozen whole-kernel corn, thawed
1 (14½-ounce) can green beans, drained
½ teaspoon lemon pepper
½ teaspoon Italian seasoning
½ cup fat-free Italian salad dressing

In a large nonstick skillet or wok, cook the chicken over medium heat until lightly browned on both sides and tender. Add the minced garlic during the last minute or two of cooking; if necessary, add ¼ cup water to keep the garlic from burning. Stir in the onion and peppers; cook about 2 minutes. Add the eggplant, zucchini, and broccoli; cook and stir for about 2 more minutes. Add the corn, green beans, seasonings, and salad dressing. Cook and stir until heated through and just crisp-tender, like Oriental stir-fry. Don't overcook. Serve with rice or pasta if desired.

SERVES 6

4 GRAMS FAT
PER SERVING

Prep	:10
Cook	:45
Stand	:00
Total	:55

HERBED BAG CHICKEN

3 tablespoons fat-free liquid margarine
1 teaspoon light olive oil
½ cup dry white wine
¼ cup chopped onion
2 large cloves garlic, chopped fine
¼ cup lemon juice
1 tablespoon Worcestershire sauce
½ teaspoon dried basil leaves
¼ teaspoon dried marjoram leaves
¼ teaspoon dried oregano leaves
6 skinless chicken breast halves (bone left in)

Preheat the oven to 350 degrees.

In a small bowl combine the margarine, olive oil, wine, onion, garlic, lemon juice, Worcestershire sauce, and spices. Mix well. Prepare a large (14 x 20-inch) oven baking bag according to the manufacturer's instructions; place the bag in a 9 x 13 x 2-inch baking pan. Place the chicken pieces, bone side down, in the bag, pour the herb mixture over, and turn the chicken so that all surfaces are coated except for the bone side. Close the bag and punch holes in the top according to instructions.

Bake 45 to 50 minutes. About halfway through the cooking time, roll the chicken around to coat the tops of the pieces again with the herb mixture. Be careful of the holes in the top—don't let them get around to the bottom or you will have a messy pan.

MARSALA CHICKEN BAKE

1 cup whole baby carrots
2 potatoes, cubed (about 2 cups)
1 small green pepper, cut into about 1-inch squares
2 boneless skinless chicken breast halves
²/₃ cup Marsala wine
1¼ teaspoons Italian seasoning

Preheat the oven to 350 degrees. Prepare a medium-size oven baking bag according to manufacturer's directions. Place in a rectangular baking dish.

Place the vegetables in the bottom of the bag, lay the chicken on top, pour the wine over, and sprinkle seasoning over all. Close the bag with provided tie and punch holes in the top according to instructions. Bake for 40 to 45 minutes or until tender.

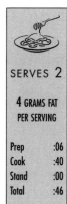

SERVES 2

4 GRAMS FAT
PER SERVING

Prep	:06
Cook	:40
Stand	:00
Total	:46

LEMON GRILLED CHICKEN

SERVES 6

4 GRAMS FAT
PER SERVING

Prep	:05
Cook	:40
Stand	3:00
Total	3:45

6 skinless chicken breast halves (bone left in)
1 cup dry white wine
½ cup lemon juice
1 teaspoon paprika
1 clove garlic, minced
1 lemon, cut into thin half-moon slices

Place the chicken in a plastic zipper-lock bag or glass bowl. Mix the remaining ingredients and pour over the chicken. Close tightly or cover and refrigerate at least 3 hours or overnight.

Prepare a fire in a charcoal grill and bring the coals to medium heat; or preheat a gas-fired grill.

Remove the chicken from the refrigerator. Drain, reserving the marinade. Discard the lemon slices.

Place the chicken pieces bone side down on an oiled grill rack and cover loosely with a piece of foil. Grill for 20 minutes. Turn the chicken, cover, and grill for another 20 minutes, brushing with the marinade 2 or 3 times.

WINE-MARINATED CHICKEN

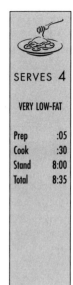

³/₄ cup white wine, such as zinfandel
⅛ cup light olive oil
2 tablespoons Dijon mustard
1½ teaspoons crushed dried rosemary
2 cloves garlic, minced
Salt and pepper (optional)
4 boneless skinless chicken breast halves

SERVES **4**

VERY LOW-FAT

Prep	:05
Cook	:30
Stand	8:00
Total	8:35

In a small mixing bowl, combine the wine, oil, mustard, rosemary, garlic, and salt and pepper if desired. Blend with a wire whisk. Reserve about ½ cup.

Place the chicken in a zipper-lock plastic bag and set the bag inside a shallow bowl. Pour the remaining marinade over the chicken. Seal the bag, turn to coat the chicken, and refrigerate overnight, turning several times to evenly coat with marinade.

Prepare a fire in a charcoal grill or preheat a gas-fired grill. Remove the chicken from the refrigerator and drain it, discarding the marinade. Arrange the chicken on an oiled grill rack and grill for about 15 minutes on each side, basting often with the reserved marinade.

BAKED MEATBALLS

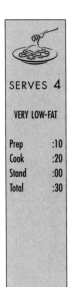

SERVES 4

VERY LOW-FAT

Prep :10
Cook :20
Stand :00
Total :30

1 pound fat-free ground turkey (or lean ground beef)
¼ cup egg substitute
½ cup fine dry bread crumbs
¼ cup skim milk
2 tablespoons finely chopped onion or 2 teaspoons instant minced onion
1 tablespoon dried parsley flakes
½ teaspoon garlic salt
½ teaspoon Worcestershire sauce
¼ teaspoon ground black pepper

Preheat the oven to 400 degrees.

In a large mixing bowl, combine the turkey, egg substitute, bread crumbs, and milk. Add all the seasonings and mix thoroughly.

On an ungreased baking sheet such as a jelly roll pan, pat the meat mixture into about a 6-inch square. With a sharp knife score almost all the way through into about 36 squares. Do not cut all the way through at this time.

Bake for 15 to 20 minutes, or until the meatballs are no longer pink in the middle. Separate the meatballs by cutting apart with a spatula or pancake turner.

Use in a sauce at this time or freeze up to 3 months. Separate before freezing.

TURKEY MEATBALLS

1 pound fat-free ground turkey
¼ cup soft bread crumbs (about ½ slice bread)
¼ cup chopped onion
¼ fat-free Parmesan cheese
¼ teaspoon garlic salt
⅛ teaspoon ground allspice

SERVES 4

VERY LOW-FAT

Prep	:10
Cook	:45
Stand	:00
Total	:55

Thoroughly mix the ground turkey with the bread crumbs, onion, Parmesan, and seasonings. Shape into the desired size meatballs. Cook in a nonstick skillet, turning often, until browned and cooked through. Serve with pasta and your favorite sauce.

Variations:

Add the meatballs to your pasta sauce after browning in the skillet and simmer for meatballs and spaghetti. Or bake instead of cooking in a skillet: Pour pasta sauce over the uncooked meatballs and bake about 40 minutes or until done.

MEAT LOAF

SERVES 6

VERY LOW-FAT

Prep   :15
Cook   :45
Stand   :00
Total   1:00

⅔ cup soft bread crumbs
1 cup skim milk
1½ pounds very lean ground turkey
½ cup egg substitute
¼ cup grated onion
1 teaspoon salt
½ teaspoon ground sage
Dash of ground black pepper
  Sauce:
3 tablespoons brown sugar
¼ cup ketchup
¼ teaspoon grated nutmeg
1 teaspoon dry mustard

Preheat the oven to 350 degrees.

In a large mixing bowl, soak the bread crumbs in the milk for about 5 minutes. Add the turkey, egg substitute, onion, salt, sage, and pepper. Mix thoroughly and shape into a loaf. Place in a meat loaf pan with a drain rack or use a regular baking dish or loaf pan.

Make the sauce: Combine the brown sugar, ketchup, nutmeg, and mustard. Pour and spread over the top of the meat loaf. Bake uncovered for 45 to 55 minutes or until done.

Note: I usually double my sauce recipe, because it is very tasty and we like a lot of sauce on our meat loaf.

TURKEY BURGER PATTIES

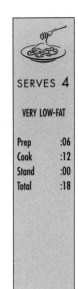

1 pound lean ground turkey
¼ cup fine dry bread crumbs
1 teaspoon lemon juice
Dash of salt
1 teaspoon ground sage
¼ teaspoon ground black pepper

SERVES 4

VERY LOW-FAT

Prep	:06
Cook	:12
Stand	:00
Total	:18

Mix the ground turkey with the bread crumbs, lemon juice, and seasonings. Shape the mixture into 4 patties about hamburger bun size. Grill as you would regular hamburgers or cook in a nonstick skillet until the desired doneness.

Turkey Cheeseburgers:

Follow the recipe for turkey burgers and top each with a slice of fat-free cheese just before the patties are done.

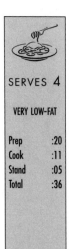

SERVES 4

VERY LOW-FAT

Prep	:20
Cook	:11
Stand	:05
Total	:36

SEAFOOD CACCIATORE

1 pound medium shrimp, shelled and deveined
³/₄ cup chopped onion
2 cloves garlic, minced
1 small green pepper, cut into thin strips (³/₄ cup)
1 (14-ounce) can tomatoes in juice
1 (8-ounce) can tomato sauce
1½ cups water
1½ teaspoons Italian seasoning
Salt and pepper to taste
⅛ teaspoon crushed red pepper flakes
1 tablespoon chicken bouillon granules (or 1 cube)
1½ cups instant rice

Spray a large nonstick skillet with olive oil cooking spray and place over medium heat. Sauté the shrimp with the onion, stirring frequently, until the onion is limp and the shrimp have turned pink. Add the garlic and green pepper and stir for 3 to 4 minutes longer, until the onion is golden.

Pour in the tomatoes with their juice, the tomato sauce, water, seasonings, and bouillon. Bring to a boil. Stir in the rice, cover, and remove from the heat. Let stand for about 5 minutes. Fluff with a fork before serving.

Chicken Cacciatore:

Substitute 1 pound of chicken tenders for the shrimp. Sauté the chicken pieces with the onion until the chicken is lightly browned; proceed with the directions above.

SHRIMP AND SPAGHETTI DELISH

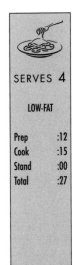

8 ounces uncooked spaghetti
¾ pound medium shrimp, shelled and deveined
2 cloves garlic, minced
½ cup dry white wine
½ teaspoon dried basil
½ teaspoon dried thyme
½ teaspoon salt
¼ teaspoon pepper

SERVES 4

LOW-FAT

Prep	:12
Cook	:15
Stand	:00
Total	:27

In a large pot of boiling water, cook the spaghetti according to package directions until tender but still firm, about 10 minutes. Drain, reserving ¼ cup of the liquid, and keep warm.

While the spaghetti is cooking, spray a nonstick skillet lightly with olive oil cooking spray and cook the shrimp over medium heat, turning often, until they turn pink, about 2 to 3 minutes. Add the garlic and stir for 30 seconds. Add the wine, basil, thyme, salt, and pepper, plus the reserved ¼ cup of pasta cooking liquid. Cover and reduce the heat to medium low and cook 2 to 3 minutes longer.

Place the hot cooked pasta in a serving dish, pour the shrimp sauce over the pasta, and toss.

ITALIAN SHRIMP SALAD

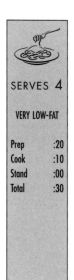

SERVES 4

VERY LOW-FAT

Prep	:20
Cook	:10
Stand	:00
Total	:30

³/₄ pound raw shrimp
1 (½-inch) slice onion
1 small slice fresh ginger
½ cup water
½ cup fat-free Italian dressing
1 (12-ounce) can artichoke hearts, quartered
2 green onions, sliced
Salt and pepper to taste (optional)

Shell and devein the shrimp. Save the shells. This sounds gross, but try it: Cook the shrimp shells, onion, and ginger in the ½ cup of water for about 5 minutes. Strain the liquid into another saucepan. Discard the above gross items.

Cook the shrimp in the seasoned liquid for 3 to 4 minutes. Let cool in the liquid, then drain, reserving the liquid.

In a salad bowl, add 2 tablespoons of shrimp liquid to the Italian dressing. Add the shrimp, artichoke hearts, green onions, and salt and pepper if desired. Toss to combine.

MARINARA SHRIMP WITH LINGUINE

8 ounces uncooked linguine
1½ cups marinara sauce (I use commercially prepared)
½ pound medium shrimp, shelled and deveined
Dash of crushed red pepper flakes
1 tablespoon lemon juice

SERVES 4

3 GRAMS FAT
PER SERVING

Prepare linguine according to package directions, leaving out any oil or butter called for. Drain and place in a serving dish.

While the linguine is cooking, heat the marinara sauce in a nonstick skillet. When hot, add the shrimp, pepper flakes (careful —not too many), and lemon juice. Cook over medium heat for 4 to 5 minutes. Pour over the linguine; toss and serve.

Prep	:10
Cook	:12
Stand	:00
Total	:22

Fennel (Finocchio)

🌿 The Romans used fennel as a means of keeping fit and trim, and indeed there is evidence to show that fennel helps break down oily and fatty foods.

During medieval times, people ate fennel seeds as an appetite suppressant.

Fennel has a licorice flavor and delicious aroma. The seeds are a complement for all kinds of breads and pastries. Sliced fresh fennel, raw or cooked, is very nice with oily fish, for instance sea bass. The feathery stalks are a wonderful garnish.

RICE-A-RONI EGGPLANT CASSEROLE

SERVES 6

4.5 GRAMS FAT
ENTIRE DISH

Prep	:25
Cook	:30
Stand	:00
Total	:55

15 fat-free saltine crackers
1 (14½-ounce) can fat-free chicken broth
1 (7.2-ounce) package herb-and-butter-flavored Rice-A-Roni
1 small eggplant
½ cup chopped onion
½ cup chopped green pepper
½ teaspoon minced garlic
¾ cup shredded fat-free mozzarella cheese
2 (4-ounce) cartons egg substitute
1 cup skim milk
1 teaspoon Italian seasoning
¼ cup Italian bread crumbs
2 tablespoons grated fat-free Parmesan cheese

Preheat the oven to 350 degrees. Spray an 8 x 12-inch baking dish with olive oil cooking spray. Line the baking dish with the crackers. Set aside.

In a saucepan, combine the chicken broth, rice, and contents of the seasoning packet. Bring to a boil, lower the heat to a simmer, and cook uncovered for 15 to 20 minutes or until the rice is tender and the liquid is absorbed.

Meanwhile, while the rice is cooking, slice the unpeeled eggplant into rounds and place in salt water (about 2 tablespoons of salt to 1 quart of water) to soak until ready to use.

In a nonstick skillet, sauté the onion, pepper, and garlic in about 2 tablespoons of water. (If using frozen onions and peppers as I did, you will not need any water; there is enough moisture in them already.) Cook just until crisp-tender; remove from the heat.

You are now ready to assemble the casserole:

Layer the rice mixture over the crackers.

Layer the onion mixture over the rice.

Layer the drained eggplant slices over the onion mixture (about 6 slices will cover).

Layer the mozzarella over the eggplant slices.

Mix the egg substitute with the milk and Italian seasoning and pour over the casserole. Sprinkle the bread crumbs and Parmesan over all. Bake uncovered for 25 to 30 minutes or until a knife inserted near the center comes out clean and the eggplant is tender.

Variation:

Substitute 6 ounces linguine, cooked according to package directions, for the rice mixture. Add 1 can of Healthy Request cream of mushroom soup blended with ¾ can of water to the linguine and omit the chicken broth.

EGGPLANT STEAKS

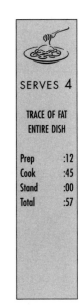

1 large eggplant
1 cup cornflake crumbs
1 teaspoon garlic pepper seasoning
¾ cup egg substitute
¼ cup skim milk
2 teaspoons grated fat-free Parmesan cheese

SERVES 4

TRACE OF FAT
ENTIRE DISH

Prep	:12
Cook	:45
Stand	:00
Total	:57

Preheat the oven to 375 degrees. Spray a large baking sheet with olive oil cooking spray.

Remove a thin lengthwise slice from opposite sides of the unpeeled eggplant, to facilitate even slicing. Cut the eggplant lengthwise into 4 or 5 slices about ¾ inch thick. Soak in salt water to cover for 10 to 15 minutes.

Mix the cornflake crumbs and the pepper seasoning in a pie plate or shallow dish. In another shallow dish, mix the egg substitute with the milk.

Drain the eggplant and pat dry with paper toweling. Dip one slice at a time in the egg and milk mixture, then coat with the crumbs. Place on the prepared baking sheet. Spray the tops of the eggplant pieces with olive oil cooking spray and sprinkle about ½ teaspoon of Parmesan over each.

Bake uncovered for 45 minutes or until lightly browned and tender.

EGGPLANT LASAGNE

SERVES 4

1 GRAM FAT
PER SERVING

Prep	:20
Cook	1:00
Stand	:06
Total	1:26

1 medium-size eggplant (about 1 pound), unpeeled, halved
  lengthwise, and sliced crosswise 1/4 inch thick
2 tablespoons lemon juice
2 (8-ounce) cans tomato sauce
1 (14-ounce) can tomatoes, drained and chopped
2 cloves garlic, minced
1/4 teaspoon crushed red pepper flakes
1 teaspoon dried oregano
1 teaspoon crushed dried basil
1/3 cup fine dry bread crumbs
1/4 cup grated fat-free Parmesan cheese
1/2 cup fat free ricotta cheese
1/4 cup shredded fat-free mozzarella cheese

Preheat the broiler. Brush the eggplant slices with lemon juice, spray both sides lightly with olive oil cooking spray, and place on a nonstick baking sheet. Broil 5 to 6 inches from the heat for 2 to 2½ minutes on each side or until golden brown.

Reduce the oven temperature to 350 degrees. In a medium-size bowl, mix together the tomato sauce, tomatoes, garlic, red pepper flakes, oregano, and basil. In a small bowl, combine the bread crumbs and Parmesan cheese.

Spoon half of the tomato sauce into a deep 1½-quart lasagne pan, sprinkle with one-third of the bread crumb mixture, and cover with a layer of eggplant. Spread ½ the ricotta cheese over the eggplant and continue to layer in the same order, ending with the tomato sauce. Scatter the mozzarella cheese over the top and bake for 45 to 55 minutes or until bubbling.

Increase the heat to broil and place the casserole in the broiler 5 to 6 inches from the heat. Broil for 1 minute or until golden brown. Let stand 5 or 6 minutes before serving.

MAKE-AHEAD EGGPLANT CASSEROLE

1 eggplant, sliced in rounds ½ inch thick
1 cup raw rice
1 cup chopped onion
1 clove garlic, minced
1 cup sliced mushrooms
1 (8-ounce) can tomato sauce
1 teaspoon dried oregano
½ teaspoon dried basil
1 cup fat-free or low-fat ricotta cheese
¼ cup skim milk
½ cup shredded fat-free mozzarella cheese
2 tablespoons grated fat-free Parmesan cheese

SERVES 6

1 GRAM FAT
PER SERVING

Prep	:10
Cook	:50
Stand	:00
Total	1:00

Place eggplant slices in salted water to cover (1 tablespoon salt to 1 quart of water) and let stand for about 15 minutes. Meanwhile, cook the rice according to package directions, omitting any oil or butter, and set aside. Drain the eggplant, place in a single layer in a nonstick skillet, and cook until crisp-tender, turning once. Transfer to a dish and set aside.

In the same nonstick skillet, sauté the onion, garlic, and mushrooms in ¼ cup of water until crisp-tender. Add the tomato sauce and herbs, scraping up browned bits from the bottom and sides of the pan. Simmer for a few minutes. Mix the ricotta cheese and milk in a separate small bowl.

Spray a 2-quart baking dish with vegetable oil cooking spray; layer the cooked rice, eggplant, ricotta, and sauce. Repeat, ending with sauce. Top with mozzarella. Sprinkle Parmesan over the mozzarella.

At this point you may cover with foil or plastic wrap and refrigerate until time to use or bake uncovered at 350 degrees for 30 to 35 minutes.

STUFFED ITALIAN-STYLE EGGPLANT

SERVES 4

SLIGHT TRACE
OF FAT

Prep   :10
Cook   :30
Stand   :00
Total   :40

1 medium-size eggplant
¼ cup chopped onion
¼ cup chopped celery
2 cloves garlic, minced
1 medium tomato, coarsely chopped
½ teaspoon dried basil
Pinch of salt and pepper (optional)
½ cup tomato sauce
2 tablespoons grated fat-free Parmesan cheese (dried sprinkle type will do)

Cut the eggplant in half lengthwise. Scoop out the pulp with a spoon, leaving about ½ inch, so you have some body to your shell. Coarsely chop the eggplant pulp. Place the shells and chopped pulp in a container with enough water to cover and about 2 tablespoons of salt. Let soak while you are preparing the stuffing, then drain in a colander before using.

Heat a nonstick skillet lightly sprayed with olive oil cooking spray. Add the onion and celery. Cook over medium heat for 2 to 3 minutes. Add the garlic and cook while stirring for about 30 seconds. Add the drained chopped eggplant, tomato, basil, and salt and pepper if desired. Mix carefully. Cover and cook 15 minutes while you preheat the oven to 400 degrees. Stir in the tomato sauce and spoon the stuffing into the eggplant shells. Sprinkle Parmesan cheese evenly over the stuffing. Place the eggplant in an ovenproof dish and bake uncovered for about 10 minutes, or until the eggplant is hot and the cheese is melted.

Eggplant Tip:

> Soaking sliced or chopped eggplant in salt water for 10 or 15 minutes before using it helps with discoloration. (I probably tell you this every time I use eggplant. This is a trick that Grandma taught me. Look how brown the water you pour off them is.)

Note: This recipe may be prepared the day before. After you fill the eggplant shells, cover them with plastic wrap and refrigerate until about 3 hours before cooking.

ITALIAN STRATA

2 cups green or red pepper strips
½ cup canned or fresh sliced mushrooms
¾ cup chopped onion
1 teaspoon Italian seasoning
½ teaspoon ground black pepper
30 low-salt fat-free soda crackers, such as Zesta or Premium
1 cup shredded fat-free mozzarella cheese
1½ cups skim milk
1 (8-ounce) carton egg substitute

SERVES 6

0 GRAMS FAT

Prep	:15
Cook	:40
Stand	:10
Total	1:05

Preheat the oven to 350 degrees. Lightly coat a 2-quart baking dish with vegetable oil cooking spray.

In a large nonstick skillet, sauté the peppers, mushrooms, onion, Italian seasoning, and black pepper in ¼ cup of water until crisp-tender.

In the prepared baking dish, layer 10 crackers, ⅓ of the vegetable mixture, and ⅓ cup of the cheese. Repeat the layers 2 more times.

In a small bowl, combine the milk and egg substitute. Pour the mixture evenly into the casserole. Bake for 35 to 40 minutes or until a knife inserted 1 inch from the center comes out clean. Let stand 10 minutes before serving.

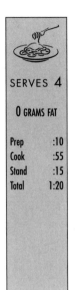

BAKED FRITTATA

SERVES 4

0 GRAMS FAT

Prep	:10
Cook	:55
Stand	:15
Total	1:20

1 small eggplant, unpeeled
1 large potato, peeled and sliced thin
1 small onion, sliced thin, separated into rings
1 small zucchini, sliced into thin rounds
1 small red or green bell pepper, chopped
2½ cups egg substitute
1 teaspoon Italian seasoning
½ teaspoon ground black pepper
Pinch of salt (optional)
1 small tomato, chopped (optional)

Slice the eggplant into thin rounds and soak in heavily salted water (1 tablespoon of salt to 1 quart of water) for 15 minutes. Drain and pat dry.

Preheat the oven to 400 degrees. Spray a quiche baking dish lightly with vegetable oil cooking spray. (Or use a 9-inch cake or pie plate.)

Spread the potatoes in the bottom of the prepared baking dish and cover with the onions. Bake uncovered for about 6 minutes. Remove from the oven; layer the zucchini over the potatoes and onions. Add a layer of the eggplant and sprinkle with the chopped bell pepper. Return to the oven and bake for another 8 minutes.

Meanwhile, in a medium mixing bowl, beat the egg substitute with a wire whisk just enough to mix well. Pour over the vegetables, sprinkle the spices over, and return to the oven for an additional 30 to 35 minutes or until set and puffy. Garnish with tomatoes if desired.

ITALIAN FRITTATA

1 cup egg substitute
Dash of salt
Dash of ground black pepper
1/4 teaspoon Italian seasoning
1/2 cup chopped onion
1/4 cup chopped green pepper
1/2 teaspoon chopped garlic
4 small zucchini, peeled and diced
2 tablespoons grated fat-free Parmesan cheese
Tomato sauce (optional)

SERVES 2

LESS THAN
1 GRAM FAT
PER SERVING

Prep	:10
Cook	:20
Stand	:00
Total	:30

In a small mixing bowl, combine the egg substitute, salt, pepper, and Italian seasoning. Blend with a whisk and set aside.

Heat a nonstick skillet; add 1/4 cup of water, the onion, green pepper, and garlic. Sauté until crisp-tender. Add the zucchini and cook for 4 to 5 minutes, over medium heat, stirring often, until the squash begins to brown. Spray lightly with vegetable oil cooking spray a couple of times to help with browning; add a little more water if needed to help soften your vegetables.

Reduce the heat to low; pour the egg substitute mixture over the vegetables in the skillet and sprinkle with Parmesan cheese. Cover and cook for 6 to 8 minutes or until set. Invert the frittata onto a plate and serve with tomato sauce if desired.

Note: I sprinkle a few pieces of chopped green onion or green pepper over the top along with the tomato sauce. It's very attractive as well as good.

ZUCCHINI-ONION QUICHE

This makes a nice brunch or ladies' luncheon dish. Serve with a green salad, garlic bread, and a nice drink of your choice.

SERVES 4

0 GRAMS FAT

Prep	:10
Cook	1:05
Stand	:15
Total	1:30

½ cup raw long-grain rice
1 cup shredded fat-free Swiss cheese or mozzarella
3 egg whites
1 medium-size onion, sliced thin
1 medium-size carrot, peeled and grated
1 medium-size zucchini, grated
1 cup low-sodium fat-free chicken broth
¼ teaspoon crumbled dried marjoram
¼ cup egg substitute
1 cup skim milk
¼ teaspoon ground black pepper

Prepare the pie shell: Cook the rice according to package directions, omitting any butter or salt. Cool. Preheat the oven to 425 degrees. Spray a 9-inch pie pan with vegetable oil cooking spray. In a medium-size bowl, mix together the rice, 2 tablespoons of the cheese, and 1 egg white. With moistened hands, press the mixture over the bottom and sides of the pan. Bake uncovered for 5 minutes. Remove and cool on a wire rack.

Prepare the filling:

In a medium-sized nonstick pan, combine the onion, carrot, zucchini, chicken broth, and marjoram; cook for about 15 minutes, until all liquid has evaporated and the vegetables are crisp-tender. Transfer to a medium-size heatproof bowl and cool to room temperature. Meanwhile, heat the oven to 350 degrees.

Lightly beat together the 2 remaining egg whites and the egg substitute; mix into the cooled vegetables along with the milk, pepper, and remaining cheese. Pour the mixture into the pie shell and bake, until the filling is puffed and set, about 20 to 25 minutes. Remove and cool for 15 minutes before serving.

STUFFED EGGPLANT ROLLS

1 large or 2 medium eggplants
½ cup chopped onion
½ cup chopped celery
¼ cup chopped green pepper
½ teaspoon Italian seasoning
1 (6-ounce) package Stovetop chicken-flavor stuffing mix
1 ¼ cups fat-free chicken broth
1 (10¾-ounce) can Healthy Request cream of mushroom soup

SERVES 4

3.25 GRAMS
FAT PER SERVING

Prep	:20
Cook	:45
Stand	:00
Total	1:05

Preheat the oven to 350 degrees. Lightly spray an 11 x 7-inch baking dish with vegetable oil cooking spray.

Remove a thin lengthwise slice from two opposite sides of the unpeeled eggplant, to faciliate even slicing. Cut the eggplant lengthwise into ¼-inch-thick slices. Select the 4 or 5 largest slices for stuffing. Place them in a bowl of salt water (about 1½ quarts of water and 2 tablespoons of salt) and let them soak while you prepare the stuffing.

Chop the remaining eggplant into small pieces; you will need 1 cup. (You may need to cut into a second eggplant.) Place the 1 cup of chopped eggplant in a nonstick skillet with ¼ cup of water, the onion, celery, green pepper, and Italian seasoning. Bring to a simmer and sauté for 5 to 8 minutes or until tender.

Meanwhile, in a mixing bowl combine the stuffing mix and its flavoring packet with 1⅔ cups of boiling water. When well moistened, pour into the skillet with the sautéed vegetables. Add ½ cup of the chicken broth and mix well. Transfer the stuffing to the mixing bowl and rinse out the skillet.

Drain the eggplant slices and place them (in batches if necessary) in the skillet with ¼ cup of additional water. Cook the slices briefly over medium heat, turning them a couple of times with a plastic spatula, until they are soft enough to roll. Remove from the heat.

Place about ¼ cup of the stuffing down the center of each eggplant slice and roll up, starting with a long end. Arrange the rolls in the prepared baking dish, seam side down; spoon the remaining stuffing around the rolls.

With a wire whisk, mix the cream of mushroom soup and remaining ¾ cup of chicken broth until blended. Pour over the rolls and stuffing. Lightly press down on the eggplant rolls to submerge them under the sauce.

Bake uncovered for 45 to 55 minutes, until lightly browned and bubbly.

FRITTATA WEDGES

SERVES 8

1.13 GRAMS
FAT PER SERVING

Prep	:10
Cook	:05
Stand	:00
Total	:15

¾ cup egg substitute
⅛ teaspoon salt (optional)
Pinch of ground black pepper
2 tablespoons minced 99% fat-free ham
1 teaspoon minced parsley

In a small bowl, combine the egg substitute, salt if desired, pepper, 1½ tablespoons of the ham and ¾ teaspoon of the parsley.

Spray a nonstick 7-inch skillet with olive oil cooking spray; place over medium-high heat for about 1 to 1½ minutes. Pour in the egg mixture and swirl around to coat the bottom of the skillet. Reduce the heat to low and cook without stirring until the top is set but still soft, 3 to 4 minutes.

Carefully slide the frittata onto a plate, then invert back into the skillet. Cook for 30 to 40 seconds, until set. Slide back onto the plate, cut into wedges, and serve hot or at room temperature. Garnish with the remaining ham and parsley. If serving at room temperature the frittata can be cooked 1 to 1½ hours ahead, cooled, covered, and left at room temperature.

Vegetables

PROVOLONE GREEN BEANS

2 cloves garlic, minced
2 (10¾-ounce) can french-cut green beans, drained
Salt and pepper to taste
4 ounces light provolone cheese, shredded

Coat a large frying pan or nonstick saucepan with olive oil cooking spray. Sauté the garlic over medium-low heat for 30 to 45 seconds, stirring constantly—be careful not to let it burn.

Place the beans in the pan and stir to coat with the garlic. Season with salt and pepper; cook until heated through. Transfer to a serving bowl. Add the provolone to the hot beans and toss. Serve immediately.

Variation:

Substitute ¼ cup grated Parmesan cheese for the provolone.

SERVES 4

LESS THAN
1 GRAM FAT
PER SERVING

Prep	:05
Cook	:04
Stand	:00
Total	:09

Basil

🌿 Basil came to America in the seventeenth century from Europe. It is an annual plant, growing up to two feet high. It needs a sunny area that has some protection from the wind. Keep the plant bushy by pinching out the center stem, allowing the side stems to bush. Also be sure to pinch off the flower buds before they open and to keep the soil moist.

Basil has a rich, peppery flavor that lends itself to Italian dishes. Use with tomato recipes—particularly spaghetti sauce—as well as pesto. You can also add the chopped leaves to almost any soup, as well as to lamb, fish, poultry, pasta, and eggs. Carrots, potatoes, and eggplant are enhanced by the use of basil. Lemon, garlic, and thyme all blend well with basil.

GREEN BEANS ITALIAN STYLE

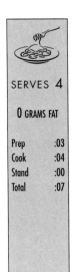

SERVES 4

0 GRAMS FAT

Prep	:03
Cook	:04
Stand	:00
Total	:07

2 (14-ounce) cans green beans with their liquid
1 (14-ounce) can Italian tomatoes, drained and chopped (reserve liquid for another use)
¼ cup chopped onion
1 small clove garlic, chopped, or ½ teaspoon garlic powder
¼ teaspon dried oregano
¼ teaspoon dried basil
Dash of pepper

In a medium saucepan bring all the ingredients to a boil, reduce the heat, and simmer for 3 to 4 minutes or until heated through. Don't cook too long—keep a little texture to your beans. Drain and transfer to serving dish.

SEASONED GREEN BEANS

SERVES 4

1.76 GRAMS FAT PER SERVING

Prep	:03
Cook	:04
Stand	:15
Total	:22

1 (14-ounce) can seasoned green beans with onions, peppers, and garlic powder
1 (2-ounce) can sliced mushrooms (or stems and pieces)
1 teaspoon olive oil
1 tablespoon red wine vinegar with Italian seasoning
⅛ teaspoon minced garlic

Pour the green beans, juice and all, into a saucepan; add the mushrooms and about ½ cup of water. Bring to a boil and cook for 3 to 4 minutes. Drain.

In a small dish or cup blend the olive oil, vinegar, and garlic. Pour over the hot beans and stir gently to coat evenly. Pour into a serving dish and serve at room temperature.

SAVORY WHITE BEANS

1 small onion, peeled and cut in half
1 celery rib, halved
1 teaspoon dried rosemary
¼ teaspoon crumbled sage
1 (16-ounce) can Great Northern white beans, drained
½ teaspoon salt (optional)
Dash of pepper

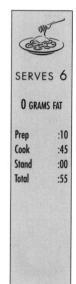

SERVES 4

VERY LOW-FAT

Prep	:10
Cook	:03
Stand	:00
Total	:13

In a nonstick skillet, sauté the onion, celery, rosemary, and sage in ¼ cup of water until tender. Add the beans, salt, and pepper. Spray lightly with olive oil cooking spray.

Cook about 3 minutes, stirring occasionally. Remove the onion and celery and discard. Drain any excess liquid. Serve hot or at room temperature.

MAKE-AHEAD BROCCOLI AND TOMATO CASSEROLE

3 (10-ounce) packages frozen broccoli, thawed and drained
2 to 3 large tomatoes, peeled and sliced about ½ inch thick
¾ teaspoon dried basil
1¼ cups fat-free sour cream
1¼ cups fat-free mayonnaise
⅔ cup grated fat-free Parmesan cheese

SERVES 6

0 GRAMS FAT

Prep	:10
Cook	:45
Stand	:00
Total	:55

Lightly spray an 11 x 7-inch baking dish with vegetable oil cooking spray. Preheat the oven to 325 degrees if you intend to cook this at time of preparation.

Place the broccoli in the prepared baking dish, top with tomato slices, and sprinkle with basil. In a small bowl, combine the sour cream, mayonnaise, and Parmesan cheese (reserve about 1 tablespoon of cheese for sprinkling over the top).

Spread the cheese mixture over the tomato slices; sprinkle with the remaining Parmesan cheese. Bake uncovered for 40 to 45 minutes or until bubbly and lightly browned.

Note: If making ahead, cover with plastic wrap and refrigerate until time to bake, following above instructions. Let stand at room temperature for 5 to 10 minutes before baking.

WINE-GLAZED CARROTS

SERVES 4

0 GRAMS FAT

Prep	:10
Cook	:15
Stand	:00
Total	:25

1 pound carrots, peeled and sliced into ½-inch rounds
1¼ cups fat-free chicken broth
Pinch each of salt and pepper
1 tablespoon sugar
¼ cup dry Marsala or sherry

Place the carrots in a nonstick skillet; add ¾ cup of the chicken broth and season with salt and pepper. Cover and cook over medium heat, stirring several times, for about 3 minutes or until the broth has almost evaporated.

Add another ½ cup of broth, cover, and continue cooking until the broth has almost evaporated once more. Sprinkle the sugar over the carrots and cook uncovered for about 2 minutes or until the carrots begin to brown, stirring carefully so as not to break them up. Add the wine and cook, stirring occasionally, until the wine evaporates to a glaze, about 2 to 3 minutes.

CAULIFLOWER FRITTI

Serve this with marinara sauce or any type of dip. Just be careful of fat grams—read your label.

1 small head cauliflower, about 1 pound, trimmed and divided into florets
1 cup all-purpose flour
¾ cup egg substitute
1 teaspoon salt (optional)
Dash of pepper
2 cups fine dry bread crumbs or cornflake crumbs

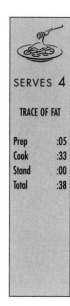

SERVES 4

TRACE OF FAT

Prep	:05
Cook	:33
Stand	:00
Total	:38

Preheat the oven to 400 degrees. Lightly coat a baking dish with vegetable oil cooking spray.

In a large saucepan of boiling salted water, parboil the cauliflower for 3 to 5 minutes or until just crisp-tender. Drain and pat dry.

Place the flour in a shallow dish or pie plate. Place the egg substitute in a second shallow dish, mixed with the salt, if using, and the pepper, and place the bread crumbs in a third.

Dredge the florets in the flour, dip in the egg substitute, and roll lightly in bread crumbs.

Arrange the cauliflower on the prepared baking sheet and lightly spray the tops with cooking spray. Bake for about 30 minutes or until golden brown.

PARMESAN EGGPLANT BAKE

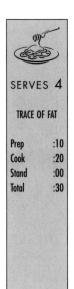

SERVES 4

TRACE OF FAT

Prep	:10
Cook	:20
Stand	:00
Total	:30

1 small eggplant (about 8 ounces)
2 tablespoons fat-free chicken broth
Salt and pepper to taste (optional)
1 cup chopped ripe tomatoes (about 2 medium), drained of juice
2 tablespoons Italian seasoned bread crumbs
2 tablespoons grated fat-free Parmesan cheese
¼ teaspoon dried basil

Preheat the oven to 400 degrees. Spray a cookie sheet or jelly roll pan with olive oil cooking spray.

Peel the eggplant and cut into ½-inch slices. Place in water to cover and add about 2 tablespoons of salt; let stand for 10 minutes.

Place the chicken broth in a shallow dish. Drain the eggplant and pat dry. Dip the slices in the broth and arrange in a single layer on the prepared baking sheet. Season with salt and pepper if desired. Bake for 12 minutes or until almost tender. Remove from the oven but leave the oven on.

Scatter the chopped tomato evenly over each slice. Combine the bread crumbs with the cheese and basil; sprinkle evenly over the tomatoes. Return the eggplant to the oven and bake 5 to 6 minutes longer, until the crumbs are lightly browned.

EGGPLANT CASSEROLE

1 large eggplant
4 slices low-fat white bread, cubed (1 gram fat per slice)
1 (5-ounce) can evaporated skim milk
¾ cup chopped onion
2 cloves garlic, minced
½ cup egg substitute
½ teaspoon salt
¼ teaspoon pepper
2 egg whites
¼ cup grated fat-free Parmesan cheese

SERVES 4

1 GRAM FAT
PER SERVING

Prep	:30
Cook	:40
Stand	:20
Total	1:30

Peel the eggplant and chop into small pieces. To keep it from discoloring, soak the eggplant in a saucepan of water with 2 tablespoons of salt. Let stand about 10 minutes. Pour the salt water off and rinse the eggplant. Cover with fresh water, bring to a boil, and cook about 10 minutes or until tender. Drain, mash the eggplant, and set aside.

Preheat the oven to 350 degrees. Spray a 1½-quart soufflé dish or baking dish with vegetable oil cooking spray.

In a medium bowl, combine the bread and milk, let stand for 10 minutes or while you are doing the next step.

In a large nonstick skillet, sauté the onion and garlic in ¼ cup of water over medium high heat, stirring constantly so as not to burn the garlic, for 5 minutes. Add the mashed eggplant, the bread-and-milk mixture, the egg substitute, salt, and pepper. Set aside.

Beat the egg whites until stiff peaks form; fold into the eggplant mixture. Pour into the prepared dish and sprinkle with Parmesan cheese.

Bake for 30 to 35 minutes or until puffed and set. Serve immediately.

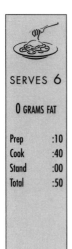

SERVES 6

0 GRAMS FAT

Prep	:10
Cook	:40
Stand	:00
Total	:50

BALSAMIC ONIONS

2 large red onions, about 1 pound
2 cups balsamic vinegar, or red wine vinegar with 1 teaspoon sugar

Preheat the oven to 350 degrees. Cut the unpeeled onions in half from root to stem end. Pour the vinegar into an 11 x 7-inch glass baking dish. Place the onions cut side down in the dish. Cover with foil.

Bake 30 to 40 minutes, until the onions are tender but still hold their shape. Remove from the pan with a spatula. Remove and discard the skins; cut each onion half into 3 wedges. Serve warm or at room temperature.

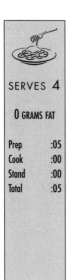

SERVES 4

0 GRAMS FAT

Prep	:05
Cook	:00
Stand	:00
Total	:05

PARMESAN PEAS

2 (10-ounce) packages frozen green peas
1 tablespoon grated fat-free Parmesan cheese
1 tablespoon lemon juice
1/2 teaspoon salt

Cook the peas according to package directions; drain. Toss with the remaining ingredients.

ROASTED GARLIC POTATOES

4 to 5 medium red potatoes, scrubbed and quartered
1 clove garlic, minced
Sprinkle of salt and pepper (optional)

SERVES 4

Preheat the oven to 350 degrees. Spray a medium-size roasting pan with olive oil cooking spray. Place the potatoes in the pan, spray lightly with cooking spray, and sprinkle garlic over the potatoes. Add salt and peper if desired.

Roast the potatoes uncovered for 45 to 50 minutes, until tender and browned.

SLIGHT TRACE
OF FAT

Prep	:05
Cook	:45
Stand	:00
Total	:50

SUMMER SQUASH ITALIANO

1 medium onion, sliced lengthwise, then cut crosswise into thin strips
1 1/4 cups frozen thin, shredded hash browns
1 medium zucchini, cut into thin strips
1 medium yellow summer squash, cut into thin strips
1 medium bell pepper, cut into thin strips
1 (14-ounce) can Italian-recipe stewed tomatoes
1 teaspoon Italian seasoning
Salt and pepper to taste (optional)

SERVES 4

SLIGHT TRACE
OF FAT

Prep	:15
Cook	:15
Stand	:00
Total	:30

In a nonstick skillet, sauté the onions and hash browns over medium-high heat until slightly browned. Add the zucchini, yellow squash, and bell pepper. Continue to sauté until crisp-tender. Add the tomatoes, juice and all, along with the Italian seasoning. Season with salt and pepper if desired. Continue to cook until heated through. Serve immediately, along with pasta or rice if desired.

SPAGHETTI SQUASH

SERVES 4

1 GRAM FAT PER SERVING

Prep	:10
Cook	1:15
Stand	:20
Total	1:45

1 large spaghetti squash (about 4 pounds)
1 medium-size yellow onion, chopped fine
³/₄ pound mushrooms, sliced
¹/₃ cup dry white wine or water
2 (8-ounce) cans tomato sauce
1 (16-ounce) can tomatoes, puréed, with their juice
2 cloves garlic, minced
¹/₄ teaspoon crumbled dried basil
¹/₄ teaspoon chopped dried rosemary
¹/₄ teaspoon crumbled dried thyme
¹/₄ teaspoon ground black pepper
3 medium-size carrots, peeled and sliced thin
2¹/₂ cups broccoli florets
1 small zucchini, sliced (about ¹/₄ pound)
¹/₄ cup grated fat-free Parmesan cheese
2 tablespoons minced parsley

Preheat the oven to 350 degrees.

Wash the squash and pierce it in several places with a fork or small knife. Set the squash on a baking sheet and bake for 1 to 1¹/₄ hours or until you can pierce it easily with a fork.

Meanwhile, in a medium-sized nonstick saucepan sprayed lightly with olive oil cooking spray, over medium heat, sauté the onion for 2 to 3 minutes. Add the mushrooms and cook, stirring, for 5 minutes. Stir in the wine, tomato sauce, tomatoes, garlic, basil, rosemary, thyme, and pepper, and simmer, covered, for 3 minutes. Add the carrots and simmer 3 to 4 minutes more. Mix in the broccoli, cook about 4 minutes; add the zucchini and cook for 2 minutes more or until crisp-tender.

When the squash is done, let it cool for 15 or 20 minutes, halve lengthwise and remove the seeds. Using a fork, scrape the flesh onto a platter. Warm up the vegetable mixture if necessary and spoon over the squash. Sprinkle with the cheese and parsley.

OVEN-FRIED ZUCCHINI

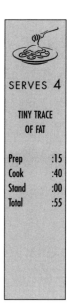

½ cup all-purpose flour
1 large zucchini, cut into 4-inch-long strips, ½ inch thick
½ cup egg substitute
¾ cup cornflake crumbs
Fat-free sour cream

SERVES 4

TINY TRACE
OF FAT

Prep	:15
Cook	:40
Stand	:00
Total	:55

Preheat the oven to 400 degrees. Lightly spray a baking sheet with vegetable oil cooking spray.

Place the flour in a bag, add the zucchini strips, and shake until all the pieces are lightly coated.

Put the egg substitute in a shallow dish and the cornflake crumbs in a separate shallow dish. Dip the zucchini strips one at a time in the egg, then in the crumbs, turning to coat them.

Arrange the zucchini on the prepared baking sheet and spray the tops lightly with cooking spray. Bake uncovered for 15 to 20 minutes or until lightly browned. Turn with a spatula and cook for another 15 minutes or until browned and crisp-looking.

Serve as a side vegetable or as an appetizer, along with fat-free sour cream for dipping.

Oven-Fried Eggplant:

Substitute a medium-sized eggplant for the zucchini. Cut into strips and soak for 15 minutes in 2 quarts of water with 2 tablespoons of salt. Drain, pat dry with a kitchen towel, and proceed as above.

ZUCCHINI WITH STUFFING

SERVES 6

0 GRAMS FAT

Prep	:20
Cook	:30
Stand	:05
Total	:55

1⅔ cups fat-free chicken broth
1 (6-ounce) package Stove Top instant stuffing mix
1 teaspoon Italian seasoning
½ cup chopped onion
½ cup chopped green pepper
½ cup chopped celery
3 medium-size zucchini

Preheat the oven to 350 degrees. Lightly coat a baking dish with vegetable oil cooking spray.

Bring the chicken broth to a boil, add the Stove Top seasoning packet and Italian seasoning, lower the heat, and simmer for about 5 minutes. Meanwhile, in a nonstick skillet, sauté the onion, pepper, and celery in ¼ cup of water until just crisp-tender. Set aside.

Stir the dry stuffing mix into the simmering broth, cover, and let stand about 5 minutes.

Cut the zucchini in half lengthwise; do not peel. Scoop out the seed section with a spoon, making a boat effect. Discard the seeds.

Mix the sautéed vegetables into the stuffing mixture. Spoon into the center of your zucchini boats, rounding them up to be quite full. Place the stuffed zucchinis into the prepared baking dish. Bake uncovered for 25 to 30 minutes or until the zucchini are tender.

Stuffed Acorn Squash:

Halve 3 small acorn squash lengthwise. Scoop out and discard the seeds. Cut a little circle off the bottom of each half so the squash will sit flat. Proceed with stuffing the squash as above; place in a baking dish or casserole, cover with foil, and bake 15 minutes longer or until the stuffing is lightly browned.

ZUCCHINI-TOMATO COMPANION

This makes a wonderful companion for almost any meal. Stir it into cooked, drained pasta of any type. Or add cooked chicken and serve over a dish of pasta.

SERVES 4

ONLY A TRACE
OF FAT
ENTIRE DISH

½ cup chopped onion
3 medium zucchini, sliced
2 medium-sized ripe tomatoes, cut into wedges
½ teaspoon dried basil leaves or 1½ teaspoons chopped fresh basil
Salt and pepper to taste

Prep	:10
Cook	:08
Stand	:00
Total	:18

   Coat a nonstick skillet lightly with olive oil cooking spray and place over medium heat. Cook the onion and zucchini, stirring occasionally, until crisp-tender. Add the tomatoes, basil, salt, and pepper. Cook until the tomatoes are thoroughly heated.

STUFFED TOMATOES

SERVES 6

2 GRAMS FAT
ENTIRE DISH

Prep	:10
Cook	:50
Stand	:00
Total	1:00

1 (10-ounce) package frozen chopped spinach
¾ cup chopped onion
2 cups soft bread crumbs
¼ cup shredded fat-free Parmesan cheese
½ teaspoon salt
⅛ teaspoon grated nutmeg
¼ cup egg substitute
6 medium-size ripe tomatoes

Preheat the oven to 350 degrees. Spray a 9-inch baking dish with olive oil cooking spray.

Cook the spinach according to package directions. Drain in a colander and squeeze dry.

In a small nonstick pan, heat ¼ cup water, add the onion, and cook for 2 to 3 minutes or until just softened.

In a medium bowl, combine the onion, spinach, bread crumbs, Parmesan cheese, salt, and nutmeg. Stir in the egg substitute and mix well.

With a sharp knife, cut off the tops of the tomato about 1 inch down. Turn the tomatoes over and gently squeeze out the juice and seeds. Use a teaspoon to scoop out the pulp, making a cup. Chop the pulp, and add to the spinach mixture. Spoon the stuffing into the tomato cups and arrange in the prepared baking dish. Spray the tops of the tomatoes with cooking spray. Bake uncovered for 35 minutes. Serve hot.

ZITI WITH BREADED TOMATOES

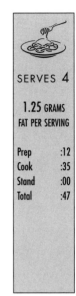

1 cup uncooked ziti
1 cup chopped onion
½ cup chopped green pepper
1 clove garlic, crushed
1 (14-ounce) can Italian-flavored stewed tomatoes
½ cup tomato juice
½ teaspoon mild pizza seasoning
1 teaspoon red wine vinegar with Italian seasoning
½ cup Italian-style bread crumbs

SERVES 4

1.25 GRAMS
FAT PER SERVING

Prep	:12
Cook	:35
Stand	:00
Total	:47

In a large pot of boiling water, cook the ziti 10 to 12 minutes or according to package directions. Drain and set aside.

In a nonstick skillet, sauté the onion, pepper, and garlic in ¼ cup water until just crisp-tender. Add the tomatoes, juice and all, 1½ cups of water, the tomato juice, pizza seasoning, and vinegar. Bring to a slow boil, lower the heat, and simmer for about 15 minutes, stirring occasionally.

Add the ziti and continue to cook for 3 to 4 minutes; stir in the bread crumbs. You may need to add ½ cup of additional water if the mixture seems too thick or dry. Simmer for 2 to 3 minutes or until nicely thickened.

SWEET AND TANGY TOMATOES

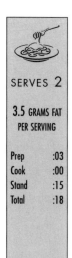

Use as a quick, easy, and pretty side dish or salad.

SERVES 2

3.5 GRAMS FAT
PER SERVING

Prep :03
Cook :00
Stand :15
Total :18

3 to 4 medium-size ripe tomatoes
1 small onion, chopped (optional)
½ teaspoon light olive oil
2 teaspoons red wine vinegar with Italian seasoning

Peel the tomatoes: Drop them into a pot of boiling water for about 60 seconds, then remove and drop into a bowl of ice water. Remove the cores with a small sharp knife and slip off the skins.

Chop the tomatoes and combine with the chopped onion in a small bowl. Pour the olive oil and vinegar over all, stirring carefully to mix well. Let stand about 15 minutes before serving, to blend the flavors.

CHEESY TOMATO SLICES

Pretty, quick, good—what more could you ask for in the summer?

SERVES 4

0 GRAMS FAT

Prep :03
Cook :00
Stand :00
Total :03

3 large ripe tomatoes
Bottled fat-free Italian dressing
¾ cup shredded fat-free Cheddar cheese
2 green onions with tops, sliced

Slice the tomatoes into 12 slices. Arrange 3 slices on each of 4 salad plates. Drizzle with dressing; sprinkle with cheese and onions.

BREADED TOMATOES AND OKRA

This is a quick, easy stovetop side dish. I don't know how Italian okra is, if at all, but I just had to include this recipe. As you can probably tell, I am writing this in the summer with lots of good okra in the garden. Hope you enjoy it. The freezer department of your grocery story has a nice crop also. I enjoy picking there more than in the garden.

SERVES 4

2 GRAMS FAT
ENTIRE DISH

Prep	:15
Cook	:40
Stand	:00
Total	:55

4 cups sliced okra, fresh or frozen
1 tablespoon vinegar
1 (14-ounce) can stewed tomatoes
1 clove garlic, minced
½ teaspoon Italian seasoning
Pinch of crushed rosemary
¼ teaspoon crushed dried oregano
2 slices bread (1 gram fat each), torn into pieces

Place the okra in a saucepan, cover with water, and add 1 tablespoon of vinegar. Boil for 2 to 4 minutes. Drain in a colander and rinse. (This gets rid of the sliminess in okra.)

In a larger saucepan, combine the undrained tomatoes and seasonings, along with the okra. Bring to a boil, lower the heat, and simmer until the okra is tender. Meanwhile, in a food processor crumb the 2 bread slices. Pour the crumbs into the okra-tomato mixture, stir carefully to blend, and simmer for about 10 minutes. Be careful not to burn.

ROASTED VEGETABLES WITH SUN-DRIED TOMATO PESTO

SERVES 4

4.5 GRAMS FAT
PER SERVING

Prep   :15
Cook   :40
Stand   :03
Total   :58

2 tablespoons balsamic vinegar
1 tablespoon olive oil
Dash each of salt and pepper
2 cups sliced red potato (½-inch-thick slices)
2 cups ½-inch-thick zucchini rounds
1 cup halved mushrooms
1 pound eggplant, cut diagonally into ½-inch-thick slices
3 tablespoons sun-dried tomato pesto (recipe page 180)

Preheat the oven to 450 degrees. Coat a cookie sheet or jelly-roll pan with vegetable oil cooking spray.

In a large mixing bowl, combine the vinegar, olive oil, salt, and pepper. Stir well. Add the potato, zucchini, mushrooms, and eggplant; coat evenly by tossing gently. Let stand 3 minutes.

Arrange half the vegetables on the prepared pan. Bake for 10 minutes; turn with a pancake turner and bake an additional 10 minutes or until tender and lightly browned.

Repeat with the remaining vegetables. Remove to a serving dish. Top with the tomato pesto and toss gently to coat. Serve warm or at room temperature.

Variation:

> Substitute sliced onion and bell pepper for the mushrooms and eggplant.

GRILLED VEGETABLES WITH VINAIGRETTE SAUCE

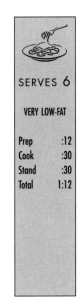

1 medium eggplant
2 medium zucchini
2 medium yellow summer squash
2 medium green or red bell peppers
   Vinaigrette Sauce:
¼ cup light olive oil
½ cup balsamic vinegar
1 teaspoon salt
¼ teaspoon black pepper
1 clove garlic, minced
2 teaspoons Italian seasoning

SERVES 6

VERY LOW-FAT

Prep	:12
Cook	:30
Stand	:30
Total	1:12

Remove a thin lengthwise slice from two opposite sides of the unpeeled eggplant to facilitate even slicing. Cut the eggplant lengthwise into ½-inch-thick slices and soak for 15 to 20 minutes in salted water (2 tablespoons of salt to 2 quarts of water).

While the eggplant is soaking, prepare the remaining vegetables: Remove strips of skin on 2 sides of the zucchini and yellow squash and slice the squash lengthwise ½ inch thick. Core and seed the peppers and cut into 1-inch-wide strips.

Make the vinaigrette sauce: In a small bowl, combine the oil, vinegar, and seasonings. Beat with a whisk until thickened.

Drain the eggplant and pat dry. Layer the eggplant, squash, and peppers in a glass dish or deep nonaluminum bowl. Pour the vinaigrette mixture over and let stand for 30 minutes.

Prepare a charcoal fire or preheat a gas grill; lightly spray the grill rack with vegetable oil cooking spray. Drain the vegetables, reserving the vinaigrette sauce. Working in batches, grill the vegetables on both sides for about 8 to 15 minutes (the eggplant will take longest), until fork tender. As the vegetables are done, return them to the dish and turn to coat again in the vinaigrette. Or cut the vegetables into bite-size pieces and toss in the sauce. Serve at room temperature.

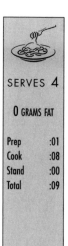

WINTER VEGETABLES VINAIGRETTE

SERVES 4

0 GRAMS FAT

Prep :01
Cook :08
Stand :00
Total :09

1 (16-ounce) package frozen brussel sprouts, carrots, and cauliflower
2 tablespoons white wine vinegar with basil
1 teaspoon hot spicy Italian seasoning

In a medium saucepan, combine the vegetables with the vinegar and seasoning. Add ½ cup of water and simmer for 7 to 8 minutes, until just crisp-tender. Drain and transfer to a serving dish.

Sauces and Toppings

TOMATO SAUCE

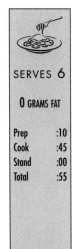

1 medium onion, chopped
2 large garlic cloves, minced
1 (30-ounce) can Italian crushed tomatoes in purée
1 teaspoon dried oregano
Pinch of crushed red pepper flakes
½ teaspoon salt

SERVES 6

0 GRAMS FAT

Prep	:10
Cook	:45
Stand	:00
Total	:55

In a large nonstick saucepan or skillet, heat ¼ cup of water and sauté the onion and garlic 2 to 3 minutes, until the onion softens. Remember, burned garlic is terrible, so watch carefully. Add the tomatoes with purée, 1 cup of water, the oregano, and pepper flakes. Bring to a boil, reduce heat to medium low, and cook partially covered for 30 minutes. Season with salt. Serve with your choice of pasta.

Bay Leaves

🌿 Bay leaves have been in use for over two thousand years. A native of Middle Eastern and Mediterranean countries, the bay laurel tree grows to over fifty feet tall in some areas of Greece. However, if grown in a small tub, it reaches a height of approximately five feet. It is very hard to grow. Your best bet is the fresh market.
Bay is a fairly powerful herb; use it with a very light hand. Use in Spanish and French soups, stews, and sauces is almost a must. Bay leaves combined with saffron, garlic, and citrus make a very nice blend. Always remove bay leaves from soups before serving.

ITALIAN TOMATO SAUCE

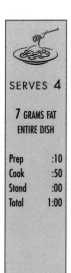

SERVES 4

7 GRAMS FAT
ENTIRE DISH

Prep	:10
Cook	:50
Stand	:00
Total	1:00

1 teaspoon olive oil
1 cup chopped onion
1 cup chopped green bell pepper
2 cloves garlic, minced
2 (16-ounce) cans whole tomatoes, undrained
2 (8-ounce) cans tomato sauce
2 teaspoons dried basil leaves
1 bay leaf
1 teaspoon salt
1 teaspoon dried oregano
¼ teaspoon ground black pepper

Heat the oil in a large saucepan and sauté the onion and green pepper for 5 minutes or until the onion is just tender. Add the garlic and stir for 45 to 60 seconds, being careful not to burn it. Stir in the remaining ingredients, breaking up the tomatoes with a fork. Bring to a boil, reduce the heat, cover, and simmer for about 45 minutes, stirring often. Remove the bay leaf before serving.

CHUNKY TOMATO SAUCE

1 teaspoon light olive oil
2 cups chopped onion
4 cloves garlic, minced
½ cup canned tomato purée
1 (16-ounce) can Italian plum tomatoes with their juice, crushed
4 sprigs parsley
12 fresh plum tomatoes, about 1½ pounds, peeled and coarsely
    chopped
½ teaspoon salt
¼ teaspoon pepper
2 tablespoons minced dried basil

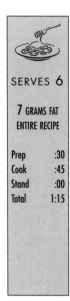

SERVES 6

7 GRAMS FAT
ENTIRE RECIPE

Prep	:30
Cook	:45
Stand	:00
Total	1:15

In a medium saucepan, heat the olive oil and sauté the onions and garlic until softened and translucent, about 10 minutes. (You may need to add ¼ cup of water—take care not to burn the garlic.)

Add the tomato purée, crushed canned tomatoes with their juice, and parsley. Simmer uncovered for about 30 minutes or until very thick. Add the chopped fresh tomatoes and cook for about 2 more minutes. Season with the salt, pepper, and basil.

Use this on pasta, pizza, or as a garnish. Use sparingly on pizza as it contains so much liquid.

SPAGHETTI SAUCE

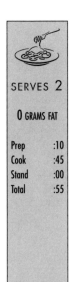

SERVES 2

0 GRAMS FAT

Prep	:10
Cook	:45
Stand	:00
Total	:55

1 ¼ cups chopped onion
¾ cup chopped green bell pepper
2 cloves garlic, chopped fine
1 (14-ounce) can Italian tomatoes with their juice
1 (8-ounce) can sliced mushrooms (optional)
1 (8-ounce) can tomato sauce
Pinch of oregano
Pinch of dried basil
Salt and pepper to taste
2 tablespoons cornstarch

In a large skillet or nonstick saucepan, sauté the onion, green pepper, and garlic in ¼ cup water for 4 to 5 minutes or until just crisp-tender.

Add the tomatoes, mushrooms if using, tomato sauce, oregano, basil, salt, and pepper. Simmer for 35 to 40 minutes.

To thicken, mix the cornstarch with ¼ cup of cold water; gradually stir into the sauce and cook 3 to 4 minutes longer.

PIZZA OR PASTA SAUCE

1 (8-ounce) can fat-free tomato sauce
1 teaspoon Italian seasoning
⅛ teaspoon garlic powder

In a small bowl, mix all ingredients. Use on pizzas.

0 GRAMS FAT

Prep	:02
Cook	:00
Stand	:00
Total	:02

GARLIC MINT SAUCE

¾ cup mint-flavored apple jelly
3 tablespoons water
3 cloves garlic, crushed

In a small saucepan, heat all ingredients over medium heat, stirring constantly until the jelly is melted. Serve with lamb.

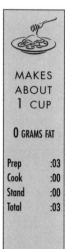

MAKES
ABOUT
1 CUP

0 GRAMS FAT

Prep	:03
Cook	:00
Stand	:00
Total	:03

WHITE WINE SAUCE

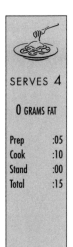

SERVES 4

0 GRAMS FAT

Prep   :05
Cook   :10
Stand   :00
Total   :15

2¼ cups fat-free chicken broth
¾ cup white wine
6 tablespoons all-purpose flour
½ cup skim milk
Salt and pepper to taste
Onion or garlic powder or Italian seasoning, if desired

In a nonstick skillet or saucepan, combine the broth and wine. Heat to boiling; reduce the heat to medium. Mix the flour and milk in a small cup or bowl until smooth; stir into the broth. Cook and stir until the mixture thickens. Thin with a little water or more wine if necessary. Add salt, pepper, and/or onion or garlic powder or Italian seasoning if desired. Don't add all together—choose one flavor to complement your chosen entree.

WHITE SAUCE OR GRAVY

SERVES 2

0 GRAMS FAT

Prep   :03
Cook   :10
Stand   :00
Total   :13

Don't tell me we can't have our gravy and eat it too!

1 (15-ounce) can fat-free chicken or beef broth
1 to 2 tablespoons flour or cornstarch
Ground pepper to taste

Measure out ¼ cup of the broth, add the flour or cornstarch, and whisk to mix until smooth.

In a saucepan, heat the remaining broth until almost simmering. Stir in the flour or cornstarch mixture; continue heatng and stirring until the gravy is thick and piping hot. Season with pepper.

GREMOLATA (LEMON PARSLEY GARNISH)

*Gremolata is a lemon rind, garlic, and parsley garnish
traditionally served with veal shanks.*

2 lemons
2 large garlic cloves, minced
⅓ cup minced fresh parsley

Grate the yellow zest from the lemons; be careful not to get any of the white pith—it is bitter. In a small bowl, combine the lemon zest, garlic, and parsley. Serve with osso buco (braised veal shanks) or with angel hair pasta (page 57).

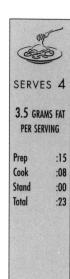

SERVES 4

3.5 GRAMS FAT
PER SERVING

Prep	:15
Cook	:08
Stand	:00
Total	:23

WHITE SAUCE MIX

1 cup unsifted all-purpose flour
2 cups nonfat dry milk powder

Mix these two ingredients together and store in a jar or zipper-lock plastic bag for up to 4 weeks.
To make sauce—depending on type needed for complementing your meal, use water, fat-free chicken broth, or beef broth—use 1 cup of desired liquid.

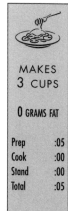

MAKES
3 CUPS

0 GRAMS FAT

Prep	:05
Cook	:00
Stand	:00
Total	:05

NONFAT WHITE SAUCE

MAKES
1 CUP

0 GRAMS FAT

Prep	:05
Cook	:08
Stand	:00
Total	:13

⅓ cup White Sauce Mix (see above)
1 cup water (or fat-free chicken broth or beef broth)
Pepper and salt to taste

In a heavy or medium-heavy saucepan, blend the sauce mix and broth or water with a wire whisk. Place over medium heat and bring to a simmer. *Do not boil—it will cause the sauce to curdle.* Stir constantly with whisk and continue to simmer until the sauce thickens—about 3 minutes. Season to taste with pepper and salt.

If you do lump your sauce, you may salvage it by straining it through a tea strainer or putting it into the blender and blending out the lumps. If you don't have a blender, try a potato masher.

HERB SAUCE

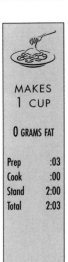

MAKES
1 CUP

0 GRAMS FAT

Prep	:03
Cook	:00
Stand	2:00
Total	2:03

1 cup plain nonfat yogurt
1 teaspoon honey
¼ teaspoon dried basil
¼ teaspoon dried tarragon
Pinch of dried dill weed
Dash of salt
1 clove garlic, crushed

Combine all the ingredients in a small bowl. Cover and refrigerate at least 2 hours to blend flavors. Serve over steamed vegetables.

SPAGHETTI SAUCE SEASONING MIX

You can keep this spaghetti mix ready and look like you have been in the kitchen all day. It only takes thirty-five minutes to create a sauce that is wonderful.

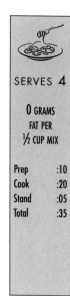

SERVES 4

0 GRAMS
FAT PER
½ CUP MIX

Prep	:10
Cook	:20
Stand	:05
Total	:35

1 cup onion flakes
1 cup parsley flakes
¼ cup crumbled dried oregano
2 tablespoons sugar
2 tablespoons dried thyme crumbled
2 tablespoons crumbled dried basil
3 teaspoons ground black pepper
4 teaspoons garlic flakes
6 large bay leaves, crumbled fine

Mix all the above ingredients in a zipper-lock plastic bag and store in a cool, dry place. Shake the bag to mix the ingredients well.

To make spaghetti sauce:

In a medium-size heavy saucepan, mix together 2 (28-ounce) cans of tomatoes, drained and chopped; 1 (6-ounce) can of tomato paste, and 1 cup of water. Stir in ½ cup of the Spaghetti Sauce Seasoning Mix. Reduce the heat and simmer for about 20 minutes; stir occasionally.

Serve over spaghetti or other pasta. Meat may be added if desired. I add chicken (white meat) or turkey. Careful—you are adding fat grams.

OREGANO PESTO

MAKES
1 CUP

3.8 GRAMS
FAT PER
(1 TABLESPOON)
SERVING

Prep	:15
Cook	:00
Stand	:00
Total	:15

2½ cups torn spinach leaves
1¾ cups fresh oregano leaves
1 cup fresh flat-leaf parsley leaves
2 tablespoons fresh Parmesan cheese
2 tablespoons pistachio nuts
4 teaspoons lemon juice
2 large cloves garlic
¼ teaspoon salt
3 tablespoons light olive oil

Place the spinach, oregano, parsley, Parmesan, nuts, lemon juice, garlic, and salt in the container of a food processor or blender. Process until smooth. With the processor on, slowly pour the oil through the food chute. Process until well blended. Pour or spoon into a container and seal tightly. Refrigerate until time of use.

SUN-DRIED TOMATO PESTO

MAKES
ABOUT
2 CUPS

0.6 GRAMS
FAT PER
(1 TABLESPOON)
SERVING

Prep	:10
Cook	:00
Stand	1:00
Total	1:10

2½ cups loose sun-dried tomatoes, not packed in oil
3 cups boiling water
2 tablespoons pine nuts, toasted
2 large cloves garlic
⅔ cup fresh basil leaves (about 1½ bunches)
2 tablespoons grated low-fat or fat-free Parmesan cheese
¼ cup fresh flat-leaf parsley leaves
3 tablespoons dry white wine

In a medium bowl, combine the tomatoes and boiling water. Let stand about 1 hour or until softened. Drain and reserve liquid.

With the food processor on, slowly put the pine nuts and garlic through the food chute and process until minced. Place the tomatoes in the container, along with the basil, cheese, and parsley; process until minced. With the processor on, pour ½ cup of the reserved tomato liquid and the wine through the food chute; process until well blended. Spoon the pesto into a covered container or zipper-lock plastic bag and store in the refrigerator.

CRUMB TOPPINGS

1 cup fine dry bread crumbs (see Note)
¼ cup liquid fat-free margarine, such as Fleischmann's
Dash of salt
1 clove garlic, crushed (optional)
1 teaspoon dried oregano (optional)
¼ teaspoon dried basil (optional)

Thoroughly mix the bread crumbs and margarine along with the salt. Use plain or add the desired seasonings. Serve over cooked, steamed, or creamed vegetables.

Note: For homemade crumbs, toast bread in a slow oven (200 to 250 degrees) until dried; process in a food processor to fine crumbs.

MAKES
1 CUP

1 GRAM FAT

Prep	:03
Cook	:00
Stand	:00
Total	:03

Desserts

APPLE LASAGNE

6 lasagne noodles
3 (20-ounce) cans apple pie filling
1 ½ cups fat-free ricotta cheese
½ cup egg substitute
¼ cup granulated sugar
½ teaspoon almond extract
¾ cup all-purpose flour
⅔ cup plus 3 tablespoons packed brown sugar
1 cup plus ¼ cup uncooked rolled oats
1 teaspoon ground cinnamon
Pinch of grated nutmeg
6 tablespoons light margarine
½ cup chopped walnuts (optional)

SERVES
10

1 GRAM FAT
PER SERVING

Prep	:15
Cook	:45
Stand	:15
Total	1:15

Preheat the oven to 350 degrees. Lightly coat a 13 x 9 x 2-inch baking dish with vegetable oil cooking spray.

Cook the lasagne noodles according to package directions; drain and set aside.

Spread half the apple pie filling (1½ cans) evenly in the prepared baking dish. Layer 3 lasagne noodles over the apples.

In a medium mixing bowl, blend the ricotta, egg substitute, granulated sugar, and almond extract. Spread evenly over the lasagne; top with the remaining 3 noodles. Layer the remaining apple pie filling over the lasagne.

In a small separate bowl, combine the flour, ⅔ cup of the brown sugar, 1 cup of oats, the cinnamon, and the nutmeg. With a pastry blender or 2 knives, cut in the margarine until crumbly. Sprinkle over the apple filling. Combine the additional ¼ cup of oats and 3 tablespoons of brown sugar with the nuts. Sprinkle over the crumb topping and spray with butter-flavored cooking spray.

Bake uncovered for 45 minutes. As with most lasagne, let stand 15 minutes before cutting and serving. You may dollop on a little fat-free sour cream and sprinkle with more brown sugar if desired.

BAKED APPLES WITH CREAM CHEESE TOPPING

SERVES 4

2 GRAMS FAT
PER SERVING

Prep	:15
Cook	:40
Stand	:00
Total	:55

4 small tart apples
¼ cup snipped pitted whole dates or raisins
2 ounces fat-free cream cheese
½ teaspoon vanilla extract
3 to 4 teaspoons skim milk
Grated nutmeg or ground cinnamon

Preheat the oven to 350 degrees. Core the apples and peel them about ¼ of the way down from the stem end. Arrange the apples in a 9-inch pie plate. Fill the centers with dates or raisins. Add ¼ cup of water to the pie plate. Bake uncovered for 40 minutes or until tender. Cool slightly.

In a small mixing bowl, stir together the cream cheese and vanilla. Stir in enough milk to make a topping of the desired consistency.

To serve, dollop the slightly cooled apples with some of the topping. Sprinkle lightly with nutmeg or cinnamon. If desired, serve some fat-free vanilla ice cream or yogurt alongside.

QUICK EASY FRUIT SALAD

I have fun finding all the new fat-free flavors. Try some.

1½ cups seedless grapes
1 (11-ounce) can mandarin orange segments, drained and chilled
1 (8-ounce) can pineapple chunks, drained and chilled
1 red apple, sliced and dipped in lemon juice
Lettuce leaves
Fat-free salad dressing

Mix the grapes, orange segments, pineapple, and apple in a bowl. Spoon onto lettuce leaves. Serve with dressing on the side and offer several different flavors.

SERVES 4

0 GRAMS FAT

Prep :05
Cook :00
Stand :00
Total :05

PINEAPPLE DESSERT

Pineapple is certainly not Italian, but in America this is very popular in Italian restaurants.

2 slices canned pineapple with 2 tablespoons of syrup
1 maraschino cherry
1 tablespoon maraschino liqueur, or more to taste

Place the pineapple slices in an individual dish or saucer. Put the cherry (I like the ones with the stem on for this) in the center hole. Add the reserved pineapple syrup and 1 tablespoon of maraschino liqueur. Refrigerate for at least 2 hours before serving.

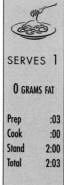

SERVES 1

0 GRAMS FAT

Prep :03
Cook :00
Stand 2:00
Total 2:03

CREAMY QUICK RICE PUDDING

SERVES 4

1 GRAM
PER SERVING

Prep	:10
Cook	:25
Stand	:30
Total	1:05

1 package vanilla-flavor sugar-free pudding and pie filling mix
(regular, not instant)
3 cups skim milk (read your label for 0 fat)
½ cup instant rice
¼ cup raisins (optional)
Ground cinnamon for garnish (optional)

In a medium-size heavy or nonstick saucepan, combine the pudding mix, milk, rice, and raisins. Bring to a boil over medium heat, stirring constantly until the pudding reaches the desired thickness, about 25 minutes. Pour into a 1-quart casserole or individual dessert dishes. To prevent a skin from forming, place plastic wrap directly on the surface of the hot pudding. Chill for 30 minutes or longer before serving. Remove the plastic wrap; sprinkle with cinnamon, if desired.

SWEET RISOTTO

1 tablespoon liquid fat-free margarine, such as Fleischmann's
3/4 cup arborio rice
1 cup boiling water
Pinch of salt (optional)
1 cup hot skim milk
1/3 cup sugar
1/8 teaspoon ground cinnamon
1/4 cup golden raisins (optional)

SERVES 2

VERY LOW-FAT
—LESS THAN
1 GRAM
PER SERVING

Prep	:10
Cook	:25
Stand	:00
Total	:35

Put the margarine in a heavy saucepan over medium heat. Add the rice; stir until well coated. Add the boiling water and salt if desired. Cook, stirring, until the water is absorbed, 5 to 6 minutes. Add the hot milk, 1/3 cup at a time; cook, stirring constantly, until the milk is absorbed, about 2 minutes after each addition.

When the rice is creamy and tender but still firm in the center, stir in the sugar, cinnamon, and raisins if using. Cook 1 to 2 minutes longer; pour into individual serving dishes. Sprinkle a touch of cinnamon over for garnish. Serve with fresh berries if desired.

RICE CAKE

SERVES 8

VERY LOW-FAT

Prep	:30
Cook	3:45
Stand	24:00
Total	28:15

This cake is like so many of us good ol' gals—it keeps improving with age. You can do it as long as 5 or 6 days ahead. Refrigerate if you're not using the next day. Take out of the refrigerator at least 4 to 6 hours before using.

1 quart skim milk
¼ teaspoon salt
2 to 3 strips lemon peel, yellow part only
1¼ cups sugar
⅓ cup raw rice, preferably Italian arborio rice
1¼ cups egg substitute
½ cup almonds, skinned, toasted, and chopped
⅓ cup candied citron or candied lemon peel, coarsely chopped
2 tablespoons rum
Fine dry unflavored bread crumbs

Put the milk, salt, lemon peel, and sugar in a medium-size saucepan and bring to a boil. As the milk comes to a boil, add the rice and mix with a wooden spoon. Cook uncovered at the lowest possible simmer for about 2¾ hours, stirring occasionally. The mixture should become a dense and pale brown mush. Most of the lemon peel will have been absorbed; remove any large visible pieces. Set aside and allow to cool.

Preheat the oven to 350 degrees.

Beat the egg substitute in a large bowl until blended. Beat in the rice and milk mush a spoonful at a time. Add the chopped almonds, candied fruit, and rum. Mix all the ingredients thoroughly.

Spray a 6-cup rectangular baking pan generously with vegetable oil cooking spray, then sprinkle the pan with bread crumbs. Shake out any excess crumbs. Pour the rice cake mixture into the pan; spread evenly. Bake uncovered for 1 hour.

Remove the cake and let cool to lukewarm. Place a platter over the pan and invert. Tap the pan a few times to loosen the cake; remove the pan. When completely cool, cover the cake and store for at least 24 hours before serving. (Do not refrigerate if serving within 24 hours.)

TIRAMISÙ

This is one of the desserts we had on our trip to New York to do research for this book, but believe me it was not low-fat. It was Fat-FULL. Erin, our guide, chose this for us to try in the dessert shoppe; it was wonderful, and so this one is for Erin.

3 cups nonfat ricotta cheese
12 ounces nonfat cream cheese (block, not tubs)
1 cup granulated sugar
½ cup Marsala wine
2 teaspoons vanilla extract
3 cups fat-free whipped topping
30 ladyfingers, separated
1½ cups strong brewed coffee
¼ cup unsweetened cocoa powder

SERVES 8

ABOUT 3.75
GRAMS FAT
PER SERVING

Prep	:20
Cook	:00
Stand	5:00
Total	5:20

In a food processor, pulse the ricotta cheese until completely smooth, then add the cream cheese, sugar, Marsala, and vanilla; pulse until just combined. Remove to a mixing bowl, fold in the whipped topping, one half at a time.

Make a tight layer of ladyfinger halves in the bottom of a 13 x 9 x 2-inch dish. Sprinkle or brush half the coffee evenly over the layer of ladyfingers. (French vanilla or another flavored coffee is great.) Cover the ladyfingers with half the cream cheese mixture, using a spoon back or spatula to smooth the filling. Next make a layer of the remaining ladyfingers over the cream cheese mixture. Sprinkle or brush the remaining coffee over this layer of ladyfingers and cover with the remaining cream cheese mixture, smoothing to the edges with a spoon or spatula.

Cover the dish with plastic wrap and refrigerate for 5 or 6 hours, or overnight. Before serving, sift cocoa powder to cover the tiramisù completely. Freezing for a few hours helps it to cut nicely.

ITALIAN CHEESECAKE

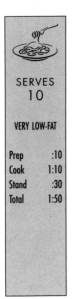

SERVES
10

VERY LOW-FAT

Prep	:10
Cook	1:10
Stand	:30
Total	1:50

Marsala Pastry:
1 cup fat-free granola
3 tablespoons sugar
1 teaspoon grated lemon zest
2 tablespoons light margarine
1 tablespoon dry Marsala or sherry
Filling:
1 pound light ricotta cheese
½ cup sugar
1 tablespoon flour
4 ounces egg substitute
¼ cup fat-free sour cream
¼ cup evaporated skim milk
1 teaspoon vanilla extract
4 egg whites

Preheat the oven to 350 degrees.

Make the pastry: In a blender or food processor, combine the granola, sugar, and lemon zest and process until fine. Add the margarine and Marsala and process until the mixture starts to come together. Line the bottom and 1 inch of the inside of a 9-inch springform pan with the pastry, patting to an even thickness.

Bake the crust for 10 minutes. Remove from the oven but leave the oven on.

Make the filling: In a large mixing bowl, combine the ricotta, sugar, and flour. Mix with a wooden spoon until well blended. Add the egg substitute, sour cream, milk, and vanilla. Beat to blend well.

In a small glass mixing bowl, free of grease, beat 4 egg whites with an electric mixer until stiff but not dry. Using a rubber spatula, fold the egg whites into the cheese mixture, one third at a time, just until mixed. Pour into the prepared pan. Bake cheesecake for 55 to 60 minutes, until the center is firm. Let cool 30 minutes. Run a knife around the edges of the pan and release the springform. Serve chilled or at room temperature.

CHOCOLATE BUDINO

This is a cake and a sauce at the same time. Quick and easy.

2 cups all-purpose flour
1½ tablespoons baking powder
¼ teaspoon salt
2 cups granulated sugar
1¾ cups unsweetened cocoa powder
1½ cups skim milk (0 fat grams—read your label)
3 tablespoons amaretto liqueur
1 tablespoon vanilla extract
2 tablespoons fat-free liquid margarine, such as Fleischmann's
1 cup packed dark brown sugar
6 tablespoons instant coffee granules

SERVES 8

1.88 GRAMS
FAT PER SERVING

Prep	:15
Cook	:30
Stand	:00
Total	:45

Preheat the oven to 350 degrees. Lightly spray an 8-inch square baking dish with vegetable oil cooking spray.

In a large mixing bowl, blend the flour, baking powder, salt, 1 cup of the granulated sugar, and ¼ cup of the cocoa. Make a well in the center.

In another bowl, blend the milk, 1 tablespoon of the amaretto, the vanilla, and the margarine with a fork. Pour into the well of the dry ingredients and stir with a fork until well blended.

Pour the batter into the prepared baking dish. Smooth the top with a spatula. Set aside while you prepare the topping.

In a medium saucepan, combine the remaining ⅔ cup of granulated sugar, 1½ cups of cocoa, 2 tablespoons of amaretto, the brown sugar, and the coffee. Stir with a wooden spoon over low heat until the sugar and cocoa are melted, 2 to 3 minutes. Remove from the heat and pour over the mixture in the baking dish. Place in the oven and bake for about 30 minutes.

Serve warm or at room temperature. Spoon into dessert dishes and top with a fat-free yogurt or ice cream or light whipped topping if desired. (Real Italians use Real cream but let's get Real—if we continue to do that we will be *Real* Fat and have Real Heart Problems.)

BISCOTTI

**MAKES
ABOUT
10
DOZEN**

0 GRAMS FAT

Prep	:30
Cook	:45
Stand	:15
Total	1:30

6 1/4 cups all-purpose flour
1 3/4 cups granulated sugar
4 teaspoons baking powder
1 1/4 cups egg substitute
1 cup skim milk
2 1/2 teaspoons vanilla extract
   Glaze (optional):
2 1/2 cups confectioners' sugar
2 to 3 tablespoons evaporated skim milk
1 1/4 teaspoons lemon juice

Preheat the oven to 350 degrees. Lightly coat 2 baking sheets with vegetable oil cooking spray.

In a large mixing bowl, combine the flour, granulated sugar, and baking powder; use a wire whisk to blend well. With a wooden spoon or your fingers, make a bowl shape or well in the center of the flour mixture. (Like Grandma used to do when baking.)

In a small separate bowl, combine the egg substitute, milk, and vanilla. Again use a wire whisk or fork to blend well. Pour the egg substitute mixture into the well in the flour mixture. Use your wooden spoon (or your fingers) to stir and mix until thoroughly combined. Dampen a kitchen towel with warm water, wring out all excess water, cover the dough, and let it rest for about 15 minutes.

With your fingers, pinch the dough into 6 pieces. You can use a spoon if you'd rather, but this is a good hands-on recipe. On a floured work space (I use a lightly floured cloth), shape each piece into a log about 3 inches by 12 inches. Roll with your hands until the logs are about 2 inches thick. Don't get carried away and get them too thin.

Place the logs at least 2 inches apart on the prepared baking sheets and bake for 35 minutes, until golden brown and firm to the touch. Remove from the oven; reduce the heat to 300 degrees. Lift the logs onto a wire rack to cool for about 15 minutes.

Place the logs on a cutting board. Slice them diagonally about 1/2 inch thick. Place the slices cut sides up on the baking sheets and return to the oven. Bake 10 minutes; turn the cookies over to the other cut side, and bake an additional 10 minutes. Turn off the heat, leaving the cookies in the oven with the door ajar to cool. Store in an airtight container or freeze until needed.

Glaze the cookies only if you are going to use them the day they are baked. While your biscotti are cooling, mix your glaze, or icing dip. In a medium-size mixing bowl combine the confectioners' sugar, evaporated milk, and lemon juice. Beat with a wire whisk until the mixture is smooth. Dip the tops of the warm cookies into the glaze and place on a wire rack or cookie sheet to dry.

Variation:

When ready to bake the first time, brush the logs with skim milk and sprinkle with sugar, or with sugar mixed with cinnamon or cocoa. Bake as directed.

MAPLE BISCOTTI

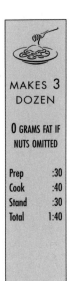

MAKES 3
DOZEN

0 GRAMS FAT IF
NUTS OMITTED

Prep	:30
Cook	:40
Stand	:30
Total	1:40

2 cups all-purpose flour
1 teaspoon baking powder
1/4 teaspoon salt
1/4 cup fat-free margarine, at room temperature
1/2 cup granulated sugar
1/2 cup firmly packed brown sugar
1/2 cup egg substitute
1 teaspoon maple flavoring
3/4 cup pecan meats, toasted (see Note) and chopped fine
    Glaze:
1 cup confectioners' sugar
1 tablespoon fat-free margarine
1/2 teaspoon maple flavoring
4 to 6 teaspoons skim milk

Preheat the oven to 350 degrees. Lightly coat a cookie sheet
with vegetable oil cooking spray.

In a small bowl, stir together the flour, baking powder, and salt;
set aside.

In a large mixing bowl, combine the 1/4 cup margarine with the
granulated and brown sugars. Beat at medium speed until very
well mixed, about 2 minutes. Continue beating while you add the
egg substitute, one half at a time, and the maple flavoring. Beat
until smooth, about 1 minute. By hand, stir in the pecans. Gently
stir in the flour mixture, mixing just until the dough is blended.

Divide the dough in half. On a lightly floured surface, roll and
stretch each portion into a 12 by 1½-inch log. Place the logs about
3 inches apart on the prepared cookie sheet. Bake for 25 minutes
or until the logs begin to crack.

Reduce the oven heat to 300 degrees. Cool the logs for 15 to
20 minutes. With a serrated knife, cut each log diagonally into
½-inch-thick slices. Lay the slices, cut side up, on the cookie
sheet. Bake, turning once, for 10 to 15 minutes or until crisp and
lightly golden brown on each side. Place on cooling racks; cool
completely.

Prepare the glaze: in a small mixer bowl, combine the confectioners' sugar, 1 tablespoon margarine, maple flavoring, and
enough milk to reach glazing consistency. Beat at medium speed
until smooth. Dip the top edge of the cooled biscotti in the glaze.

Place the dipped biscotti on waxed-paper-lined cookie sheets. Refrigerate until the glaze is hardened, about 1 hour. Store biscotti in an airtight container.

Note: To toast pecans, spread them evenly in a shallow baking pan. Bake at 350 degrees, stirring once, for 4 to 5 minutes or until lightly browned. Cool completely.

GRANOLA BISCOTTI

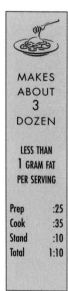

1 1/3 cups all-purpose flour
1 teaspoon baking powder
1/2 teaspoon baking soda
1/4 teaspoon salt
3/4 cup fat-free margarine, at room temperature
3/4 cup sugar
1/4 teaspoon almond extract
1/2 cup egg substitute
3/4 cup reduced-fat granola, with fruit (raisins, apples, etc.)

MAKES
ABOUT
3
DOZEN

LESS THAN
1 GRAM FAT
PER SERVING

Prep	:25
Cook	:35
Stand	:10
Total	1:10

Preheat the oven to 325 degrees. Lightly spray a cookie sheet with vegetable oil cooking spray.

Combine the flour, baking powder, soda, and salt in a medium-size mixing bowl and whisk until thoroughly mixed. Set aside.

In a large mixing bowl, with an electric mixer, cream the margarine and sugar together; beat in the almond extract and egg substitute. Gradually beat in the flour mixture and granola.

Turn out onto a lightly floured surface and divide in half. With floured hands, shape each piece into a log about 12 inches long and 1½ inches wide. Place on the prepared cookie sheet.

Bake 25 minutes or until golden brown. Place the cookie sheet on a wire rack; cool for 5 minutes. With a wide spatula transfer the logs to a cutting board; with a serrated knife slice diagonally about 3/4 inch thick.

Place the slices, cut side up, on the cookie sheet and bake for 5 minutes. Turn the cookies over and bake 5 minutes longer. Cool on the wire rack (they harden as they cool). Store in an airtight container.

ZUCCHINI BARS

MAKES
1 ½
DOZEN

0 GRAMS FAT

Prep	:25
Cook	:35
Stand	:00
Total	1:00

½ cup fat-free margarine, at room temperature
1 ½ cups packed brown sugar
1 teaspoon vanilla extract
½ cup egg substitute
2 cups all-purpose or whole wheat flour
2 teaspoons baking soda
¼ teaspoon ground cinnamon
½ teaspoon grated nutmeg
¼ teaspoon ground cloves
1 ½ cups shredded zucchini
1 cup golden raisins
  Glaze:
1 ½ cups confectioners' sugar
2 tablespoons fat-free margarine, at room temperature
1 to 2 teaspoons lemon juice

Preheat the oven to 350 degrees. Lightly coat a 13 x 9 x 2-inch baking dish with vegetable oil cooking spray.

In a large mixing bowl, cream the margarine and brown sugar together until fluffy. Beat in the vanilla and egg substitute. In a smaller bowl, combine the flour, baking soda, cinnamon, nutmeg, and cloves; stir with a whisk until well blended. Add the flour mixture to the creamed mixture and blend thoroughly with a wooden spoon. Stir in the zucchini and raisins.

Turn the dough into the prepared pan and smooth the top with a spatula. Bake 25 to 35 minutes or until a wooden pick inserted near the center comes out clean.

Meanwhile, prepare the glaze: Mix the sugar and margarine until blended. Stir in the lemon juice, 1 teaspoon at a time, until smooth and of a desired consistency.

Spread the glaze on the cake while it is still warm. Cut into bars when cool.

ZABAGLIONE

You must have a double boiler or its equivalent for this dish. It cannot be cooked over direct heat.

1 cup egg substitute
¼ cup granulated sugar
½ cup dry Marsala

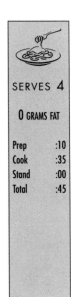

SERVES **4**

0 GRAMS FAT

Prep	:10
Cook	:35
Stand	:00
Total	:45

Place the egg substitute and sugar in the top part of a double boiler and whip with a wire whisk or electric mixer until creamy.

Bring the water to a simmer—not a boil—in the bottom of the double boiler. Place the pan with the egg mixture over the lower pan, keeping the water at a simmer. Add the Marsala and continue beating. The mixture will begin to foam and then swell into a light soft mass. It is ready when it forms soft mounds.

Spoon into pretty goblets, cups, or champagne glasses and serve immediately.

LEMON ICE

SERVES 5

0 GRAMS FAT

Prep	:10
Cook	:10
Stand	:35
Total	:55

6 cups water
3½ cups sugar
2 tablespoons grated lemon rind
1¼ cups lemon juice
¼ cup orange liqueur (optional)

Bring the water to a boil in a large saucepan; stir in the sugar until dissolved. Remove from the heat; allow to cool. Add the lemon rind and juice and the liqueur if desired. Freeze in a hand-crank or electric ice-cream freezer, following the manufacturer's directions. You may also freeze the mixture in ice trays in the freezer, stirring occasionally.

ICED WINE DELIGHT

SERVES 4

0 GRAMS FAT

Prep	:05
Cook	:03
Stand	6:00
Total	6:08

3 cups water
1½ cups sugar
3 cups white zinfandel wine

In a large saucepan, bring the water, sugar, and 1½ cups of the wine to a boil, stirring constantly until the sugar dissolves. Reduce the heat and simmer for about 3 minutes.

Cool to room temperature. Add the remaining wine; stir to blend. Pour into a shallow metal container and freeze in the freezer compartment of the refrigerator.

Stir well every 30 minutes until firm, about 6 hours. Allow to stand at room temperature for about 4 minutes; stir and serve. A mint leaf or slice of lime is a nice garnish. Be sure to use a pretty stemmed dish, maybe even a wineglass.

QUICK FROZEN DESSERT

Adjust this recipe to the number of people you're serving. The quantities of coffee and whisky can be regulated according to taste.

2 scoops fat-free vanilla ice cream
2 teaspoons ground espresso coffee beans
(or powdered in a blender)
1 tablespoon Scotch whisky

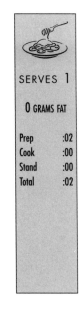

SERVES 1

0 GRAMS FAT

Prep   :02
Cook   :00
Stand   :00
Total   :02

Spoon the ice cream into a pretty individual serving dish; sprinkle with espresso and pour the whisky over all.

Variation:

I also like to use a coffee liqueur such as Kahlúa. You may add a small dollop of whipped topping and a cherry for festive holidays or entertaining.

LEMON SAUCE

½ cup sugar
2 tablespoons cornstarch
1¼ cups water
¼ cup lemon juice
½ teaspoon lemon zest (grated lemon peel)

SERVES 6

0 GRAMS FAT

Prep   :05
Cook   :03
Stand   :00
Total   :08

In a small heavy saucepan, combine the sugar and cornstarch; gradually stir in the water and lemon juice. Set over medium heat and bring to a boil. Immediately reduce the heat to low and cook, stirring constantly, until the sauce has thickened and is clear, about 2 or 3 minutes.

Remove from the heat, cool, and stir in the lemon zest. Store in a tightly covered container for up to 1 week.

Index

METRIC EQUIVALENCIES

LIQUID AND DRY MEASURE EQUIVALENCIES

Customary	Metric
¼ teaspoon	1.25 milliliters
½ teaspoon	2.5 milliliters
1 teaspoon	5 milliliters
1 tablespoon	15 milliliters
1 fluid ounce	30 milliliters
¼ cup	60 milliliters
⅓ cup	80 milliliters
½ cup	120 milliliters
1 cup	240 milliliters
1 pint (2 cups)	480 milliliters
1 quart (4 cups)	960 milliliters (.96 liter)
1 gallon (4 quarts)	3.84 liters
1 ounce (by weight)	28 grams
¼ pound (4 ounces)	114 grams
1 pound (16 ounces)	454 grams
2.2 pounds	1 kilogram (1000 grams)

OVEN-TEMPERATURE EQUIVALENCIES

Description	°Fahrenheit	°Celsius
Cool	200	90
Very slow	250	120
Slow	300–325	150–160
Moderately slow	325–350	160–180
Moderate	350–375	180–190
Moderately hot	375–400	190–200
Hot	400–450	200–230
Very hot	450–500	230–260